MINDFUL MOMENTUM

Navigating Procrastination and Overthinking

SUSHANT RAJPUT

BlueRose ONE.com
Stories Matter
NewDelhi • London

BLUEROSE PUBLISHERS
India | U.K.

For permissions requests or inquiries regarding this publication, please contact:

BLUEROSE PUBLISHERS
www.BlueRoseONE.com
info@bluerosepublishers.com
+91 8882 898 898
+4407342408967

ISBN: 978-93-6783-879-2

Cover Design: Shubham
Typesetting: Sagar

First Edition: December 2024

"Mindful Momentum" offers a well structured approach to tackle complex issues around procrastination and overthinking through simple exercises and practical techniques. A must-read for those seeking to improve their mental resilience"

Sangeetha V, Associate Director,
Cognizant Technology Solutions.

"It's a great book if you often feel stuck or stressed and want a simple plan to build better habits and feel more in control of your day-to-day life."

Vishal Jain,
Executive Director, JP Morgan

The book covers all the aspects of mindfulness in relation to diverse domains, and respective fraternity. To sum up in a line, it highlights the indispensable worth of Mindfulness as 'I take a VOW to be happy in NOW'.

Archana Kapoor Nagpal
ICF Certified Life Coach | Child Psychologist | NLP &Mindfulness Coach| L&D Soft Skills Trainer| POSH TTT

Loved it ! A Life Changing Guide to Regaining Control! The practice of mindfulness shifts chronic stress to peaceful focus. Sushant's insightful explanations and actionable techniques on Procrastination & overthinking will surely help the readers into a transformational journey.

Dr. Shekhar Doddagoudar
Agri Business Professional

More than just theory, this book provides clear, actionable steps to help readers achieve greater clarity, balance, and productivity. Its combination of empathy and practical advice makes it an invaluable resource for anyone looking to break free from overthinking/procrastination and navigate life's challenges with a fresh perspective.

Pavan Kannuri
Vice President, BNY Mellon

Acknowledgements

I have always lived by the understanding of how important it is to learn from others and be thankful for the experiences that shape our lives. Without the help and encouragement of many people, this book would not have been possible, and for that, I am incredibly thankful. It is only right to acknowledge and appreciate the numerous people who shared their thoughts and ideas with me as I embarked on the journey of writing this book.

First and foremost, I want to thank my parents, who are in their heavenly abode. Their teachings and values have molded me into a person of character, helping me achieve success both professionally and personally. When I began contemplating the topic for my next book, it was just a couple of months after my mother had passed away. I struggled to decide what to write about, as my mind often drifted to the loss of my mother, filled with memories and experiences we shared together.

However, after a few days, while watching a video on lessons we learn from our mothers, I was reminded of how my mother lived her life. One of the key aspects

I recalled was her ability to never overthink. Whether faced with a challenge, a problem, or a financial need, she always remained focused on finding solutions rather than dwelling on obstacles.

She was a solution-oriented person and never dwelled on the problems. That realization struck me profoundly—most of us tend to overthink everything. Even during her battle with cancer, in her final days, I never saw her succumb to anxiety, blame, or overthinking.

She never questioned, "*Why is this happening to me?*" Instead, she would say, "*If the outcome is predetermined, don't disturb the process by overthinking. Instead, focus on participating in the journey and let things unfold as they are meant to. Often, the outcome is beyond our control; it's better to prepare ourselves for the worst.*"

These invaluable life lessons from her became the genesis of this book. Being mindful is not an innate trait but a skill that can be practiced and implemented to become a better version of ourselves while leading a more meaningful life.

This is also a gentle reminder to all of us to express gratitude to our parents. Knowingly or unknowingly, they impart life's most profound lessons. Particularly, they teach us how to be mindful of what we say, do, and hear—skills that significantly help in curbing overthinking and procrastination.

I extend my heartfelt thanks to my family members, friends, colleagues, and respected authors who have provided invaluable insights into human behaviour, shaping my understanding of people. A special mention goes to my teachers, to whom I will always be grateful for helping me approach life's challenges and experiences with a holistic perspective, rather than confining myself to narrow thinking.

Thank you, Sanchita Lohot, for your constant inputs and support for this book, just as you did with my previous one.

Lastly, I offer my profound salutations to Lord Mahadev, who has stood by me through the highs and lows of my professional and personal journey. His divine presence has always been a guiding force.

Preface

Have you ever found yourself staring at your computer screen, knowing exactly what you need to do, but somehow unable to start? Or perhaps you've stayed awake at night, replaying the same scenario over and over in your mind, each version more stressful than the last?

If so, you're not alone. Procrastination and overthinking are common challenges that many people face in their daily lives. These twin troubles can feel like an inescapable loop, feeding off each other and creating a cycle that is difficult to break.

But what if there was a way to interrupt this cycle? What if a simple shift in mindset could help you tackle these issues head-on?

Imagine this: It's Monday morning, and you have a major project due at the end of the week. Instead of diving into your work, you find yourself scrolling through social media, checking emails, and doing just about anything except the task at hand.

As the hours slip by, a familiar sense of dread begins to creep in. You start to think about how little time you have left, which only makes you feel more overwhelmed and less capable of starting. This is procrastination in action.

Now consider another scenario: You have an important decision to make, and instead of weighing your options and making a choice, you find yourself stuck in a loop of endless analysis. You go over every possible outcome, consider every potential consequence, and second-guess yourself at every turn. The more you think about it, the harder it becomes to make a decision. This is the paralysis of overthinking.

These situations are all too familiar for many of us. Procrastination and overthinking are not just minor inconveniences; they can have a significant impact on our lives. They can affect our productivity, our mental health, and our overall sense of well-being. They can prevent us from reaching our goals and living our lives to the fullest. But why do we fall into these traps, and more importantly, how can we escape them?

At the root of both procrastination and overthinking is often a lack of mindfulness. Mindfulness, simply put, is the practice of being fully present in the moment, without judgment. It's about paying attention to your thoughts, feelings, and surroundings in a way that is both aware and accepting. When we are mindful, we are better able to recognize the patterns of procrastination and overthinking as they arise, and we can take steps to address them before they spiral out of control. Mindfulness is rooted in ancient meditation practices but has been embraced by modern psychology for its numerous mental health benefits.

Imagine being able to approach your tasks with a clear, calm mind, free from the clutter of over-analysis and the pressure of looming deadlines. Mindfulness offers this possibility. It helps us break the cycle of avoidance by encouraging us to face our tasks with curiosity and acceptance, rather than fear and resistance. When we practice mindfulness, we become more aware of our habits and triggers, allowing us to respond to challenges with greater clarity and intention.

Consider the case of procrastination. When we procrastinate, we are often trying to avoid an unpleasant task or the discomfort that comes with it. We might distract ourselves with other activities to temporarily escape that discomfort. However, this avoidance only serves to increase our anxiety and stress in the long run. By practicing mindfulness, we can learn to acknowledge the discomfort without letting it dictate our actions. We can recognize the urge to procrastinate as it arises, and gently guide ourselves back to the task at hand. This doesn't mean that the discomfort magically disappears, but it does mean that we can face it with a greater sense of calm and control.

Similarly, mindfulness can be a powerful tool in combating overthinking. When we overthink, we are often caught up in a loop of worry and rumination. We replay past events or imagine future scenarios, trying to predict and control every possible outcome. This can be exhausting and paralyzing. Mindfulness helps us to break free from this loop by bringing our attention back to the present moment. It reminds us that the future is uncertain and that our attempts to control it through overthinking are often futile. By staying grounded in the present, we can make decisions with greater clarity and confidence, without being weighed down by unnecessary worry.

The benefits of mindfulness go beyond just addressing procrastination and overthinking. Research has shown that mindfulness can improve our overall mental health, reduce stress, and enhance our ability to focus and concentrate. It can help us to develop greater emotional resilience and to respond to challenges with a sense of calmness. In short, mindfulness can help us to live more fulfilling and balanced lives.

But how do we cultivate mindfulness in our daily lives? The good news is that mindfulness is a skill that can be developed through practice. There are many different techniques and exercises that can help you to become more mindful. These can range from formal practices like meditation to informal practices like mindful walking or eating. The key is to find what works best for you and to make it a regular part of your routine.

For example, you might start your day with a short mindfulness meditation. This could involve sitting quietly and focusing on your breath, noticing the sensation of each inhale and exhale. When your mind wanders, as it inevitably will, you simply bring your attention back to your breath, without judgment. This simple practice can set a calm and focused tone for the rest of your day.

Throughout the day, you can incorporate mindfulness into your routine in small ways. You might take a few moments to really savor your morning coffee, paying attention to the taste, the smell, and the warmth of the cup in your hands. Or you might take a few mindful breaths before starting a new task, to center yourself and bring your full attention to the task at hand.

As you begin to integrate mindfulness into your life, you may start to notice subtle shifts in your behavior and mindset. You might find that you are less prone to procrastination, because you are better able to face the discomfort that comes with certain tasks. You might find that you are less caught up in overthinking, because you are more grounded in the present moment. Over time, these small shifts can lead to significant improvements in your productivity, your mental health, and your overall sense of well-being.

As we embark on this journey together, remember that change doesn't happen overnight. Breaking the habits of procrastination and overthinking requires patience, practice, and persistence. But with mindfulness as your guide, you'll discover a path to greater productivity, peace, and fulfillment.

So, are you ready to take the first step toward a more mindful and productive life? Let's begin this journey together, one mindful moment at a time.

Contents

Chapter 1

Understanding Procrastination and Overthinking

"Only put off until tomorrow what you are willing to die having left undone."

– Pablo Picasso

Procrastination. It's a word we all know too well. We've all been there, staring at a task we need to complete but finding ourselves doing anything but that task. Maybe it's cleaning your entire house when you should be working on a report, or binge-watching a TV series the night before an important exam. But what exactly is procrastination, and why do we do it?

In his TED Talk, "Inside the Mind of a Master Procrastinator," Tim Urban offers a fascinating glimpse into the decision making process of a procrastinator. He introduces us to two key players in this mental drama: the Rational Decision-Maker (RDM) and the Instant Gratification Monkey.

Urban explains that in both procrastinators and non-procrastinators, the RDM is the one typically in charge, steering the ship toward productive, meaningful activities. However, procrastinators have an additional companion in their minds: the Instant Gratification Monkey. This mischievous creature has a knack for derailing even the best-laid plans.

When the RDM tries to make a sensible, productive decision—like working on a project or studying—the Instant Gratification Monkey jumps in, hijacking the process and steering attention toward anything more enjoyable and immediately rewarding. Instead of tackling that important task, you might find yourself watching YouTube videos, reorganizing your bookshelf, or endlessly scrolling through social media.

The Instant Gratification Monkey is driven purely by the pursuit of easy and fun activities, with no concern for the past or future. It lives entirely in the present moment, and its sole focus is on what feels good right now. On the other hand, the RDM understands the importance of balancing short-term pleasure with long-term goals. The RDM knows that sometimes it's necessary to engage in less enjoyable activities for the sake of future success and fulfillment. This clash between the monkey and the decision-maker leads to what Urban calls "the Dark Playground."

The Dark Playground is a mental space every procrastinator knows all too well. It's where you indulge in leisure activities at times when you should be working. The problem is that the fun experienced in the Dark Playground is tainted by guilt, anxiety, and self-loathing because it's not truly earned. Instead of feeling relaxed, you're weighed down by the knowledge that you're avoiding what really needs to be done.

As the deadline looms closer, the procrastinator's brain finally triggers the arrival of the Panic Monster. This is the moment when the impending consequences of not completing a task become so severe that the Instant Gratification Monkey runs off in fear, and the RDM is finally able to take control. The Panic Monster forces the procrastinator to buckle down and focus, often resulting in a frantic, last-minute sprint to complete the task just in time.

While the Panic Monster might save the day occasionally, relying on it comes with its own set of problems—like unnecessary stress and the risk of subpar work.

Understanding this dynamic is key to overcoming procrastination, as it highlights the importance of developing strategies to keep the Instant Gratification Monkey in check and avoid the chaos of the Dark Playground altogether.

Procrastination isn't just about laziness or poor time management. It's a complex behavior with deep psychological and emotional roots. It's influenced by various factors which can make it a challenging habit to break. At its core, procrastination is a way of coping with challenging emotions and negative moods induced by certain tasks. These emotions can include boredom, anxiety, insecurity, frustration, resentment, and self-doubt.

A study by Tice and Baumeister (1997) examined procrastination as a form of mood regulation. They found that students often procrastinate to avoid tasks that elicit negative emotions. However, this avoidance typically leads to short-term mood improvement but long-term negative consequences. For instance, a student who finds studying for exams boring and stressful might procrastinate by watching TV or socializing. While this provides temporary relief from boredom and stress, it results in increased anxiety and lower exam scores when the student is forced to cram at the last minute.

One of the main psychological factors behind procrastination is the concept of immediate gratification. Our brains are wired to seek out rewards and pleasure, and sometimes, the immediate reward of a distraction (like social media or a snack) can seem more appealing than the long-term reward of completing a task. This is especially true when the task at hand feels difficult, boring, or stressful.

Another factor is fear of failure. When we procrastinate, we avoid the possibility of failing. By not starting a task, we protect ourselves from the potential disappointment and judgment that might come with doing poorly. This fear can be paralyzing and often leads to a cycle of avoidance and guilt.

Perfectionism also plays a significant role in procrastination. When we set unrealistically high standards for ourselves, we might delay starting a task because we fear it won't be perfect. This can lead to a lot of stress and anxiety, further contributing to procrastination.

Emotionally, procrastination often ties into our need to regulate feelings. Tasks that evoke negative emotions such as anxiety, boredom, or frustration can lead us to procrastinate as a way of avoiding those feelings. However, this avoidance usually only provides temporary relief. The task still needs to be done, and the negative emotions can build up over time, creating a vicious cycle.

A study by Solomon and Rothblum (1984) investigated procrastination among college students and its impact on academic performance. The researchers found that students who procrastinated reported higher levels of stress and lower academic achievement. The students cited anxiety about their performance, fear of failure, and a lack of motivation as primary reasons for their procrastination. For example, a student might avoid starting a term paper because the thought of writing it is overwhelming, causing anxiety and stress. This avoidance temporarily reduces anxiety but ultimately leads to last-minute cramming, poor-quality work, and heightened stress.

In some cases, procrastination can be a way to rebel against expectations or authority. If we feel that a task is imposed upon us by someone else, procrastinating can be a form of passive resistance. This is often seen in workplaces or schools, where tasks might feel obligatory rather than chosen.

To understand how procrastination manifests, let's look at some common thought patterns and behaviors associated with it.

One typical pattern is overestimation of future time. We often convince ourselves that we'll have more time to complete a task in the future than we do right now. This leads to statements like, "I'll start tomorrow," or "I'll have more energy to do this later." This faulty thinking ignores the fact that future time is just as limited as present time, and often, we don't feel any more motivated later than we do now.

Another common behavior is task avoidance. This can take many forms, such as doing less important tasks (like organizing your desk) instead of the critical one (like writing that report). This kind of procrastination is sneaky because it feels productive, even though the main task is still being avoided.

Distraction seeking is another behavior to watch out for. This includes things like constantly checking your phone, scrolling through social media, or finding other small, immediate pleasures to fill the time instead of working on the main task.

"Worry pretends to be necessary
but serves no useful purpose."

Eckhart Tolle

Overthinking, on the other hand, is like a mental hamster wheel—once you start, it's hard to stop. Do you often find yourself lying in bed at night, trying to fall asleep, but your mind is racing? You're replaying a conversation you had earlier in the day, analyzing every word, wondering if you said the wrong thing. Or perhaps you're worrying about an upcoming presentation, imagining all the things that could go wrong. The more you think, the more anxious you become. This is overthinking, and it's something many of us are all too familiar with.

You find yourself trapped in a loop of repetitive and unproductive thoughts. It can prevent you from making decisions, taking action, or even enjoying the present moment. Understanding the psychological and emotional factors that contribute to overthinking can help you break free from its grip and find a sense of peace and clarity.

Overthinking is often driven by a desire for control and certainty. When faced with uncertainty or potential risks, our brains go into overdrive, trying to predict and prepare for every possible outcome. This might sound like a good strategy, but it often leads to analysis paralysis, where we become so bogged down in details and "what-ifs" that we can't make a decision or take action.

Emotional factors also play a significant role. Anxiety, stress, and low self-esteem can fuel overthinking. When we're anxious, our brains are on high alert, constantly scanning for threats. This can lead to excessive rumination, where we replay events in our minds, trying to identify what went wrong or how we could have done things differently. Similarly, if we lack confidence in our abilities, we might overthink to compensate, scrutinizing every detail to avoid making mistakes.

Overthinking is characterized by a variety of common thought patterns and behaviors that can trap individuals in a cycle of worry and indecision. Understanding these patterns and behaviors is crucial for identifying and addressing overthinking.

One prevalent thought pattern associated with overthinking is catastrophizing, where individuals automatically assume the worst-case scenario. This pattern leads to an exaggerated sense of fear and anxiety, as the mind fixates on unlikely but disastrous outcomes. Catastrophizing often results in a heightened state of alertness and stress, making it difficult to focus on the present moment or take constructive action.

Another common thought pattern is rumination, which involves repeatedly thinking about past events, mistakes, or decisions. This relentless mental replay can prevent individuals from moving forward, as they become stuck in a loop of regret and self-blame. Rumination often leads to feelings of helplessness and can exacerbate symptoms of anxiety and depression.

Analysis paralysis is a behavior closely linked to overthinking, where individuals become so caught up in evaluating options and outcomes that they are unable to make a decision or take action. This paralysis stems from a fear of making the wrong choice and the desire to ensure that every decision is perfect. As a result, individuals remain stuck in a cycle of overanalysis, unable to move forward.

Mind-reading is another thought pattern that contributes to overthinking. This involves assuming that you know what others are thinking or feeling, often without any concrete evidence. Mind-reading can lead to unnecessary worry about how others perceive you or your actions, and can create social anxiety and self-doubt.

Behaviors associated with overthinking include seeking excessive reassurance from others. Individuals may constantly ask for validation or advice to alleviate their anxiety and gain a sense of certainty. However, this behavior often reinforces the overthinking cycle, as they become dependent on external validation rather than trusting their own judgment.

Avoidance is a common behavior where individuals steer clear of situations, tasks, or decisions that trigger overthinking. While avoidance may provide short-term comfort, it prevents individuals from confronting their fears and developing coping strategies. Over time, avoidance can lead to missed opportunities and increased anxiety.

Also, overpreparation is a behavior where individuals spend excessive time and effort preparing for a task or decision in an attempt to mitigate potential problems. While preparation is generally positive, overpreparation can become counterproductive, consuming valuable time and energy and delaying action.

By recognizing the psychological and emotional factors that contribute to this behavior, you can develop strategies to address it. Remember, these are common challenges, and it's okay to struggle with them. The key is to approach it with mindfulness and self-compassion, taking small steps towards building healthier mental habits.

Recognise Your Patterns

Understanding procrastination and overthinking is the first step towards overcoming it. Look out for these signs:

How to Catch Yourself Procrastinating

1. **Making Excuses**: If you find yourself frequently rationalizing why you can't start a task ("I work better under pressure," "I need a break first," "I don't have everything I need"), you're likely procrastinating.
2. **Distraction Habits**: Pay attention to how often you're seeking out distractions, like checking your phone or getting up to get a snack. If these activities become a regular way

to avoid your work, it’s a clear sign of procrastination.

3. **Feeling Overwhelmed**: If a task feels so big that you don’t know where to start, and this feeling leads you to avoid it altogether, you’re procrastinating. Breaking the task into smaller, manageable steps can help mitigate this.
4. **Unproductive Busyness**: If you’re constantly busy but not making progress on your main tasks, you’re likely procrastinating by focusing on less important activities.

How to Know You're Overthinking

1. **Repetitive Thoughts**: If you find yourself repeatedly going over the same thoughts or scenarios without reaching a resolution, it's a sign of overthinking.
2. **Excessive Analysis**: Constantly analyzing every detail of a situation or decision, even minor ones, indicates overthinking. You may spend more time thinking than taking action.
3. **Physical Symptoms**: Overthinking can manifest in physical symptoms like tension headaches, muscle tightness, or stomach discomfort. Your body reacts to the stress caused by incessant rumination.
4. **Sleep Disturbances**: Overthinking can disrupt your sleep patterns, leading to insomnia

or restless sleep. Your mind remains active, making it hard to relax and fall asleep.

5. **Negative Impact on Mood**: Overthinking often leads to heightened anxiety, stress, or mood swings. You may feel irritable, anxious, or emotionally drained due to excessive mental activity.

Resources

Articles:

1. Why Wait? The Science Behind Procrastination
2. A Psychologist Tells You How To Identify Your Procrastination Style
3. 10 Signs You're Overthinking (And What To Do About It)

Books:

1. Eat That Frog!: 21 Great Ways to Stop Procrastinating and Get More Done in Less Time
2. Atomic Habits
3. Get Out of My Head
4. Don't Believe Everything You Think

Key takeaways

- Procrastination is a coping mechanism for avoiding tasks that evoke negative emotions like anxiety, boredom, or fear of failure.

- The Rational Decision-Maker is often overpowered by the Instant Gratification Monkey, leading to distractions and avoidance.
- The Dark Playground is a guilt-ridden mental space where unearned leisure replaces productive work.
- The Panic Monster appears as deadlines approach, forcing last-minute action but creating stress and suboptimal results.
- Procrastination is fueled by fear of failure, perfectionism, overestimation of future time, and mood regulation.
- Overthinking involves repetitive and unproductive thoughts, often driven by anxiety, uncertainty, and a need for control.
- Behaviors like reassurance-seeking, avoidance, and overpreparation prevent action and worsen anxiety.
- Procrastination and overthinking can cause physical symptoms like headaches, sleep disturbances, and emotional exhaustion.
- Awareness of these patterns and small actionable steps, like breaking tasks into manageable parts and practicing mindfulness, can help overcome these tendencies.

Chapter 2

The Mindfulness Approach

"Realize deeply that the present moment is all you ever have. Make the Now the primary focus of your life."
– Eckhart Tolle, Author of "The Power of Now"

Imagine a day where you wake up feeling calm, focused, and ready to tackle your tasks without the usual dread or anxiety. You move through your to-do list with ease, and when you hit a roadblock, you face it with patience and clarity instead of frustration and stress. This is not an unreachable ideal but a potential reality through the practice of mindfulness.

Mindfulness is the practice of paying deliberate attention to the present moment, with an attitude of openness, curiosity, and non-judgment. At its core, mindfulness involves two key components: awareness and acceptance. Awareness is about noticing what is happening in your thoughts, feelings, and surroundings at any given moment. Acceptance means acknowledging these experiences without trying to change them or react to them impulsively.

Jon Kabat-Zinn, a pioneer in the field of mindfulness, defines it as "the awareness that arises from paying attention, on purpose, in the present moment, and non-judgmentally."

The principles of mindfulness can be summarized as follows:

1. **Non-judgment**: Observing your thoughts and feelings without labeling them as good or bad.
2. **Patience**: Understanding that things unfold in their own time.
3. **Beginner's Mind**: Seeing things as if for the first time, with curiosity and openness.
4. **Trust**: Trusting yourself and your feelings.
5. **Non-striving**: Being present without trying to achieve any specific goal.
6. **Acceptance**: Accepting things as they are.
7. **Letting Go**: Releasing attachment to certain thoughts and feelings.

Mindfulness has profound physiological effects on the body and brain. Practicing it leads to significant changes in brain structure and function. Research using magnetic resonance imaging (MRI) has demonstrated that mindfulness meditation increases gray matter density in regions associated with memory, learning, emotional regulation, and self-awareness, such as the hippocampus and prefrontal cortex. These changes suggest enhanced cognitive functions and better emotional control. Moreover, mindfulness practice reduces activity in the amygdala, the brain's center for fear and stress responses. This reduction correlates with decreased stress and anxiety levels, indicating that mindfulness helps modulate the body's response to stressors. Enhanced connectivity between the prefrontal cortex and the amygdala improves the brain's ability to regulate emotional responses, fostering a calmer and more focused mental state.

Mindfulness practice also affects neurotransmitter levels, which play a vital role in regulating mood and behavior. Dopamine, associated with pleasure and reward, increases during mindfulness meditation. Higher dopamine levels can enhance motivation and feelings of contentment. Additionally, mindfulness has been found to increase levels of gamma-aminobutyric acid (GABA), a neurotransmitter that inhibits neural activity and promotes calmness. Increased GABA levels help reduce anxiety and promote relaxation.

Practicing mindfulness influences the endocrine system, leading to hormonal changes that support well-being. One significant effect is the reduction of cortisol levels, the primary stress hormone. High cortisol levels are linked to numerous health issues, including hypertension, impaired cognitive function, and a weakened immune response. By lowering cortisol levels, mindfulness helps mitigate these negative health impacts and promotes a sense of relaxation and calm.

Additionally, mindfulness can increase serotonin production, a neurotransmitter associated with feelings of well-being and happiness. Enhanced serotonin levels help improve mood and reduce symptoms of depression and anxiety.

So how does mindfulness play a role in overcoming procrastination and overthinking? Procrastination, as we've seen, often stems from an attempt to avoid discomfort, whether it's the anxiety associated with starting a task, the fear of failure, or the boredom of a repetitive activity. Mindfulness helps by allowing us to acknowledge and accept these uncomfortable feelings without letting them dictate our actions.

A study published in the journal *'Learning and Individual Differences'* explored the relationship between mindfulness and academic procrastination among university students. The researchers found that students who practiced mindfulness reported lower levels of procrastination. This was attributed to the fact that mindfulness helped students become more aware of their avoidance behaviors and allowed them to address their tasks with greater focus and less emotional reactivity.

In practice, mindfulness can help break the cycle of procrastination. For example, let's consider a student who often finds himself putting off assignments until the last minute. When he starts practicing mindfulness, he begins by setting aside a few minutes each day to sit quietly and focus on his breath. He notices when his mind starts to wander to thoughts of his assignments and the anxiety they bring. Instead of trying to push these thoughts away, he acknowledges them and brings his focus back to his breath. Over time, he finds that he's able to start his assignments with less resistance and more focus.

Overthinking involves getting stuck in a loop of repetitive thoughts, often focused on the past or future. This can lead to increased anxiety, stress, and difficulty making decisions. Mindfulness, by contrast, anchors us in the present moment, helping to break the cycle of rumination and worry.

Research published in *Behaviour Research and Therapy* examined the effects of mindfulness on rumination and worry. The study involved participants who were prone to anxiety and overthinking. They were divided into two groups: one that received mindfulness training and another that did not. The results showed that the mindfulness group experienced significant reductions in rumination and worry compared to the control group. This was because mindfulness helped participants develop greater awareness of their thoughts and emotions, allowing them to respond more calmly and effectively.

The researchers concluded that mindfulness training can be a valuable tool for individuals who struggle with overthinking, as it promotes mental clarity and reduces the tendency to get stuck in negative thought loops.

Mindfulness-Based Cognitive Therapy (MBCT) is an approach that combines mindfulness practices with cognitive therapy techniques to help individuals manage chronic stress and prevent relapse in depression. Research published in the *Journal of Consulting and Clinical Psychology* found that MBCT significantly reduced symptoms of anxiety and depression in participants, many of whom struggled with overthinking.

In a practical sense, mindfulness can help an employee who constantly replays conversations and worries about how she is perceived by her colleagues. When she starts practicing mindfulness, she learns to observe her thoughts without judgment. She notices the pattern of her overthinking and, instead of engaging with these thoughts, she gently redirects her attention to the present moment, whether it's her breath, the sounds around her, or the sensation of her feet on the ground. This practice helps her to break the cycle of rumination and feel more grounded and present in her daily life.

In today's fast-paced world, maintaining mental clarity, emotional stability, and productivity can be challenging. Mindfulness, the practice of staying present and fully engaging with the current moment, offers a powerful tool to address these challenges.

Mental clarity refers to the state of having a clear, focused, and organized mind. It is essential for effective decision-making, problem-solving, and overall cognitive functioning. Mindfulness helps achieve mental clarity by reducing cognitive clutter and enhancing attention.

A study published in *Psychological Science* examined the impact of mindfulness meditation on cognitive function. Researchers found that participants who engaged in a short, 10-minute mindfulness meditation session demonstrated improved attention and working memory compared to those who did not meditate. The study concluded that mindfulness meditation helps clear mental distractions and enhances cognitive performance.

Mindfulness enhances emotional regulation by helping individuals become more aware of their emotions and how they influence behavior. By observing emotions without judgment, individuals can respond to them more skillfully, rather than reacting impulsively.

Research published in the journal *Emotion*, explored the impact of mindfulness on emotional regulation. The study involved participants with high levels of anxiety and depression who were randomly assigned to a mindfulness-based stress reduction (MBSR) program or a control group. The results showed that those in the MBSR group experienced significant reductions in anxiety and depression symptoms, as well as improved emotional regulation skills. The researchers concluded that mindfulness training helps individuals develop greater awareness and acceptance of their emotions, leading to better emotional control and resilience.

Productivity is not just about doing more but also about doing the right things efficiently and effectively, and to achieve this, mindfulness serves as a helpful tool. Mindfulness boosts productivity by improving focus, reducing distractions, and enhancing stress management. When individuals are mindful, they are more present and engaged in their tasks, which increases the quality of work.

A study published in the *Journal of Occupational Health Psychology* investigated the effects of mindfulness on workplace productivity. The study involved employees from various industries who participated in an eight-week mindfulness-based intervention program. The results showed that participants experienced significant improvements in their ability to focus, manage stress, and regulate emotions. These changes translated into increased productivity, better job performance, and enhanced overall well-being.

Resources

Link of the articles are added on sushantrajput.co.in

Key Takeaways

- Mindfulness emphasizes living in the present moment with awareness and acceptance, as outlined by principles such as non-judgment, patience, and letting go.
- Research shows mindfulness enhances cognitive function by improving memory, focus, and emotional regulation, while reducing stress and anxiety.
- Practicing mindfulness helps overcome procrastination by addressing avoidance behaviors and reducing emotional reactivity.
- Overthinking can be alleviated through mindfulness, which anchors individuals in the present and breaks cycles of repetitive, negative thought patterns.
- Mindfulness-Based Cognitive Therapy (MBCT) combines mindfulness and cognitive techniques to reduce symptoms of anxiety and depression effectively.
- Studies show mindfulness boosts productivity by improving focus, reducing distractions, and enhancing stress management in personal and professional settings.

- Regular mindfulness practice fosters mental clarity, emotional resilience, and improved decision-making, making it a powerful tool for overall well-being.

Chapter 3

Mindfulness Techniques

A student today may face a myriad of challenges that can hinder their ability to practice mindfulness. Academic pressure is one of the most significant obstacles. With the constant demands of coursework, assignments, exams, and extracurricular activities, students can often find themselves in a perpetual state of stress and anxiety. This relentless pressure to perform and succeed academically leaves little room for mental relaxation or introspection. The fear of failure and the need to meet high expectations can create a mental environment that is anything but conducive to mindfulness.

Furthermore, the social environment in schools and colleges is bustling with activities and peer interactions that can be both a source of support and distraction. The constant engagement with friends, social media, and various clubs or organizations often leads to an over-packed schedule, making it difficult for students to find quiet moments for mindfulness practice. The lure of digital devices and the addictive nature of social media further compound this issue, as students may find it hard to disconnect from their screens and focus on being present in the moment.

For professionals, the primary challenge to practicing mindfulness is the demanding nature of the modern workplace. High workloads, tight deadlines, and the pressure to meet performance targets create a high-stress environment that leaves little room for mental downtime. Employees often feel a constant sense of urgency and the need to be perpetually productive, which can make the idea of taking a few minutes for mindfulness seem impractical or even indulgent.

Additionally, workplace culture can significantly impact an employee's ability to engage in mindfulness practices. In environments where long hours and constant availability are expected, taking breaks or engaging in activities that are perceived as non-productive can be stigmatized. This cultural pressure can deter employees from prioritizing their mental well-being. Moreover, the blurring of boundaries between work and personal life, especially with the rise of remote work, makes it challenging for employees to find a clear separation where they can practice mindfulness. The continuous juggling of professional responsibilities and personal commitments often leads to burnout, making it even more difficult for employees to incorporate mindfulness into their daily routines.

Addressing the challenges of incorporating mindfulness into daily life requires intentional strategies and easy-to-follow techniques. Setting aside just a few minutes each day to focus on practicing can make mindfulness an accessible and sustainable habit. By making these small, manageable changes, individuals can experience the profound benefits of mindfulness and enhanced overall well-being. Integrating mindfulness into daily life doesn't need to be complicated; it just requires a bit of intention and consistency.

Mindfulness isn't always about sitting in a quiet room and meditating for hours. It's about being fully present and engaged in whatever you're doing, moment by moment.

However, in our fast-paced world, it's easy to get caught up in the whirlwind of activities and distractions. Reflect on these questions honestly and see if any resonate with your daily experience.

1. **Did you allow yourself to wake up without looking at your phone?**

Think about your mornings. Do you reach for your phone first thing, checking emails, messages, or social media before you even get out of bed? This habit can set a tone of distraction for your entire day.

2. **Do you eat your meals while watching TV or scrolling through your phone?**

Consider your eating habits. Are you truly tasting and enjoying your food, or are you multitasking and barely noticing what you're consuming? Mindful eating means savoring each bite and being aware of the flavors, textures, and smells of your food.

3. **When was the last time you sat quietly and just focused on your breathing?**

Reflect on your day. How often do you take a moment to simply breathe and be present? If you can't remember, it might be a sign that you're not giving yourself enough time to just be.

4. **Do you often feel overwhelmed or anxious without knowing why?**

Pay attention to your emotions. If you find yourself frequently stressed or anxious without a clear reason, it could indicate a lack of mindfulness.

5. **Are you aware of the physical sensations in your body throughout the day?**

Notice your body. Do you realize when your shoulders are tense, or when you're holding your breath? Being mindful means being in tune with your body and understanding how your emotions affect your physical state.

6. **Do you find it difficult to focus on one task at a time?**

Assess your focus. Are you constantly multitasking, jumping from one activity to another without completing any? Mindfulness is about dedicating your full attention to one task at a time.

7. **When someone is talking to you, are you fully listening, or are you thinking about your response?**

Consider your conversations. Are you genuinely listening to others, or are you mentally preparing what you'll say next? Mindful communication means being fully present and engaged with the person you're interacting with.

8. **Do you often forget what someone just said to you?**

Reflect on your attentiveness. If you frequently find yourself asking people to repeat themselves, it might be a sign that you're not truly paying attention to them in the moment.

9. **Do you allow yourself time to relax without feeling guilty?**

Think about your downtime. When you take a break, do you feel guilty or anxious about not being productive? Mindfulness includes recognizing the importance of rest and allowing yourself to enjoy it without negative feelings.

Recognizing these signs will bring you closer to incorporating more mindfulness into your life. It's not about being perfect, but about becoming more aware of how you're living day to day. If you noticed that many of these questions apply to you, don't worry! It's a common experience in our busy world. The good news is that mindfulness practices can help you bring more presence and awareness into your daily routine.

Before diving into specific techniques, it's important to cultivate the right mindset for practicing mindfulness. At its core, mindfulness is about paying attention to the present moment with a non-judgmental, open, and accepting attitude. It involves being aware of your thoughts, feelings, bodily sensations, and the surrounding environment.

Think of mindfulness as cultivating a garden. Just as a gardener patiently tends to their plants, we must patiently nurture our minds. This involves cultivating awareness, acceptance, and a sense of curiosity about our inner experiences. With these elements in place, we can create a fertile ground for mindfulness to flourish.

Here are some key principles to keep in mind:

1. **Non-Judgment**: Approach your thoughts and feelings without labeling them as good or bad. Simply observe them as they are.
2. **Patience**: Understand that mindfulness is a practice that takes time to develop. Be patient with yourself as you learn and grow.

3. **Beginner's Mind**: Embrace each moment as if you are experiencing it for the first time. This helps you stay open to new insights and perspectives.
4. **Trust**: Trust in your own experience and intuition. Mindfulness is a personal journey, and your experiences are valid.
5. **Non-Striving**: Focus on being rather than doing. Mindfulness is not about achieving a specific outcome but about being present in the moment.
6. **Acceptance**: Accept things as they are, without trying to change or resist them. This doesn't mean you have to like everything, but it means acknowledging reality.

With these principles in mind, you can create a solid foundation for your mindfulness practice. Whether you're stuck in a cycle of procrastination or can't stop overthinking, mindfulness offers practical ways to bring peace and focus into your daily life. Let's dive in and discover how some simple, enjoyable practices can make a big difference.

Guided meditations are a fantastic way to start your mindfulness journey. They're like having a gentle guide leading you through the process, helping you stay focused and present. Whether you're a student facing exam stress or an employee juggling multiple tasks, guided meditations can help you center yourself and find calm amidst the chaosing to enhance their mindfulness practice. Let's explore some simple yet effective guided meditations that you can easily incorporate into your daily routine.

Breath Awareness Meditation

This meditation is a classic and one of the simplest ways to start practicing mindfulness. It helps you anchor your mind in the present moment by focusing on your breath.

1. Find a comfortable seat. You can sit on a chair with your feet flat on the ground or cross-legged on a cushion.
2. Close your eyes and take a few deep breaths, in through your nose and out through your mouth.
3. Now, let your breath return to its natural rhythm and simply focus on the sensation of breathing. Feel the air enter and leave your nostrils, notice the rise and fall of your chest or abdomen.
4. Whenever your mind wanders (which it will!), gently bring your attention back to your breath without judgment.
5. Continue this for about 5-10 minutes. Open your eyes slowly when you're ready.

Remember, the goal isn't to stop thinking but to keep bringing your focus back to your breath whenever you notice your mind has wandered. This meditation helps clear mental clutter, making it easier to focus on tasks without being overwhelmed by overthinking or procrastination.

Loving-Kindness Meditation

This meditation focuses on cultivating compassion and positive feelings towards yourself and others, which can counteract negative self-talk and stress.

1. Sit comfortably and close your eyes. Take a few deep breaths to settle in.
2. Begin by focusing on yourself. Silently repeat these phrases: "May I be happy. May I be healthy. May I be safe. May I live with ease."
3. After a few minutes, think of someone you love and repeat the phrases for them: "May you be happy. May you be healthy. May you be safe. May you live with ease."
4. Gradually extend these wishes to others: a neutral person, someone you have difficulties with, and eventually all beings.
5. Spend about 15-20 minutes in this practice, opening your eyes slowly when you're done.

Feel free to personalize the phrases. The key is to generate warm, kind feelings towards yourself and others.

Body Scan Meditation

The body scan is a great way to check in with yourself, helping you become more aware of physical sensations and reducing stress.

1. Lie down on your back with your legs uncrossed and your arms by your sides. Close your eyes and take a few deep breaths.
2. Begin by focusing on your toes. Notice any sensations: warmth, coolness, tingling, or even numbness.
3. Slowly move your attention up your body, part by part: feet, calves, knees, thighs, hips, abdomen, chest, hands, arms, shoulders, neck, and finally your head.
4. Spend a few moments on each part, acknowledging any sensations without judgment and letting go of tension as you exhale.
5. Finish by bringing your attention to your entire body as a whole, appreciating it for carrying you through life.

This meditation can take 15-30 minutes and is a fantastic way to relax deeply and connect with your body. This meditation grounds you and helps reduce the mental noise associated with overthinking, promoting relaxation and focus.

Mindfulness-Based Stress Reduction (MBSR) is a well-established program designed to reduce stress and enhance well-being through mindfulness practices. These techniques are grounded in scientific research and are highly effective in managing stress. Here are some MBSR techniques that can easily fit into your daily life, providing you with tools to handle stress more effectively.

The STOP Technique

The STOP technique is a quick and practical way to interrupt stress and bring yourself back to the present moment.

1. **S – Stop**: Whatever you're doing, just pause for a moment.
2. **T – Take a Breath**: Take a deep breath and feel the air enter and leave your lungs.
3. **O – Observe**: Notice what is happening inside and around you. What are you thinking? What are you feeling? What physical sensations do you notice?
4. **P – Proceed**: With a sense of awareness, continue with whatever you were doing.

This technique creates a mental pause, allowing you to approach situations with a clear and calm mind, which is particularly useful when you're feeling overwhelmed or stuck in procrastination.

The Three-Minute Breathing Space

This technique is a mini-meditation designed to bring you back to the present moment, perfect for a quick reset during a busy day.

Awareness: Take a moment to notice what is happening right now. What thoughts are going through your mind? What emotions are you feeling? What bodily sensations are present?

Breathing: Direct your full attention to your breathing. Feel the sensation of each breath coming in and going out.

Expanding: Expand your awareness outward from your breath to include your whole body, as if your whole body is breathing.

This technique helps ground you in the present moment, reducing the stress that fuels procrastination and overthinking.

Mindfulness doesn't have to be a separate activity from your daily routine. By making small, intentional changes, you can cultivate a more mindful lifestyle that enhances your overall well-being. Here are a few practical strategies to seamlessly incorporate mindfulness into your everyday routine.

Mindful Morning Routine

Starting your day with mindfulness sets a positive tone and prepares you to handle whatever comes your way.

Wake Up Gently: Instead of reaching for your phone first thing in the morning, take a few deep breaths and gently stretch your body.

Morning Rituals: As you brush your teeth, shower, or have breakfast, focus on the sensory experiences – the taste of your toothpaste, the warmth of the water, the texture of your food.

Set Intentions: Take a moment to set a positive intention for the day. It could be something like, "Today, I will be kind to myself" or "I will approach challenges with patience."

A mindful morning routine can energize you and provide the focus needed to tackle your tasks for the day, reducing procrastination.

Mindful Breaks

Taking short breaks throughout your day to reset your mind and body can be incredibly beneficial.

1. Set a timer to remind you to take a break every hour.
2. During your break, step away from your desk and take a few deep breaths.
3. Stretch your body and pay attention to how it feels.
4. If possible, take a short walk outside and focus on your surroundings.

Regular mindful breaks prevent burnout and maintain a steady level of productivity and mental clarity, helping to counteract overthinking and procrastination.

Mindful Eating

Transform your meals into opportunities for mindfulness, making eating a more enjoyable and present experience.

1. Before eating, take a moment to appreciate the food in front of you.
2. Notice the colors, textures, and smells of your meal.
3. Take small bites and chew slowly, paying attention to the taste and sensation of each bite.
4. Put your fork down between bites and breathe.

Mindful eating helps break the cycle of mindless snacking often triggered by stress or overthinking, promoting healthier eating habits and a more mindful approach to daily activities.

There you go!

Mindfulness is an accessible, practical approach that can be seamlessly woven into your daily routine. Start small. Pick one or two areas where you feel you're lacking mindfulness and focus on those. Intentional actions can make a significant difference, enhancing your well-being and bringing a deeper sense of presence and purpose to your daily activities. Over time, these small changes can lead to a more mindful, peaceful, and fulfilling life.

Workbook for Progress Tracking

Regularly reflecting on your mindfulness practice helps you stay motivated and aware of your progress. Use this space below to track your daily experiences and insights.

Weekly Reflections:

1. How did starting your day mindfully affect your mood and productivity?

____

2. What mindfulness practices did you try this week?

____

3. What challenges did you encounter?

____

4. How did mindfulness impact your procrastination and overthinking?

____

Monthly Progress Check:

1. How has your mindfulness practice evolved over the past month?

____

2. What benefits have you noticed in your daily life?

____

3. What areas do you still want to improve?

____

Resources

Books:

1. "Wherever You Go, There You Are" by Jon Kabat-Zinn
2. "The Miracle of Mindfulness" by Thich Nhat Hanh
3. "Radical Acceptance" by Tara Brach

Apps:

1. Headspace
2. Calm
3. Insight Timer

Key Takeaways

- Mindfulness is the practice of being fully present and engaged in the moment.
- Students face challenges like academic pressure, social distractions, and digital devices, which hinder their ability to practice mindfulness.
- Professionals struggle with high workloads, tight deadlines, and blurred work-life boundaries, leading to stress and burnout.
- Mindfulness involves cultivating a non-judgmental and accepting attitude, focusing on the present, and nurturing patience and trust in one's experiences.

- Techniques like guided meditations, the STOP technique, and mindful eating help integrate mindfulness into daily life.
- Starting small and being consistent can improve focus, reduce stress, and enhance overall well-being.

Chapter 4

Time Management and Goal Setting

Time management and goal setting are foundational skills that significantly impact our lives, shaping not only our productivity but also our overall sense of well-being and fulfillment. In a world where demands and distractions are constantly vying for our attention, mastering these skills becomes essential for achieving personal and professional success.

At its core, time management is about making intentional choices on how to use our limited time effectively. Good time management allows us to prioritize tasks, set boundaries, and allocate time for what truly matters. Without it, we can easily become overwhelmed, missing deadlines and opportunities.

Effective time management reduces stress by creating a sense of order and predictability in our daily routines. When we manage our time well, we can balance work, personal life, and leisure activities, leading to a more harmonious and satisfying life.

When it comes to goal setting, it mainly provides direction and purpose. Goals act as a roadmap, guiding our actions and decisions toward desired outcomes. By setting clear, achievable goals, we give ourselves a sense of direction and motivation. Goals help us to focus our efforts and resources on what is most important, preventing us from wasting time on unproductive activities.

They also serve as benchmarks for measuring progress and success, allowing us to celebrate achievements and stay motivated.

Many of us find ourselves caught in the cycle of putting things off and ruminating over decisions, which can be incredibly draining and unproductive. The illusion of ample time leads procrastinators to the reality of wasted hours.

Procrastination is a formidable barrier to effective time management, often stemming from deeper psychological patterns and habits that can be tough to break.

One of the core challenges for procrastinators is the tendency to underestimate the time required to complete tasks. This cognitive distortion, known as the planning fallacy, leads to last-minute rushes and subpar work quality. When you finally sit down to tackle that looming project, panic sets in.

The pressure is immense, and the quality of your output often suffers because there isn't enough time to refine your work. This cycle of delay and stress can create a perpetual sense of inadequacy and frustration.

Moreover, procrastinators often struggle with prioritization. When faced with multiple tasks, it's easier to choose the ones that are either more enjoyable or less demanding, pushing the more critical or challenging tasks to the bottom of the list. This mismanagement of priorities can result in important deadlines being missed and key responsibilities neglected. The overwhelming sense of having too much to do but not knowing where to start creates a paralyzing effect, further delaying progress.

Distractions are another significant hurdle. In the age of digital connectivity, the lure of social media, online games, and endless internet browsing can be irresistible. For a procrastinator, these distractions provide a convenient escape from tasks that seem daunting or unappealing.

The constant ping of notifications and the temptation to check your phone can fragment your attention, making it difficult to focus on a single task for an extended period. This scattered attention leads to a lack of progress and a growing to-do list that feels impossible to tackle.

Overthinking, on the other hand, often starts with the pressure to make the "perfect" decision. You might find yourself questioning every goal you consider. Is this the right goal? What if I fail? What if this goal isn't ambitious enough? What if it's too ambitious? These questions swirl around, creating a fog of uncertainty. The desire for perfection can paralyze you, leading to procrastination.

Instead of confidently setting a goal, you may spend hours, days, or even weeks mulling over possibilities without making any concrete decisions.

Another hurdle for overthinkers is the tendency to foresee every possible obstacle. While it's good to anticipate challenges, overthinkers often magnify these obstacles to the point where they seem insurmountable. You might envision every way things could go wrong, from lack of resources to unforeseen setbacks.

This negative foresight can make any goal seem impossible, discouraging you from even trying. The fear of failure looms large, and rather than risking that failure, you might avoid setting goals altogether.

Even once a goal is set, an overthinker's journey is far from over. You might find yourself obsessing over every detail of the plan to achieve your goal. Instead of taking action, you spend excessive time planning, researching, and refining your approach.

While planning is crucial, over-planning can become a form of procrastination. The fear of making a mistake keeps you in a cycle of preparation, preventing you from moving forward.

Moreover, overthinkers often grapple with self-doubt. You might question your abilities and worthiness to achieve the goal. This internal dialogue can be incredibly discouraging. You may tell yourself that you're not skilled enough, not smart enough, or not dedicated enough. This negative self-talk erodes your confidence, making it hard to believe in your capacity to achieve your goals.

The good news is that mindfulness can be a powerful ally in your quest to manage time more effectively and set meaningful goals. Primarily, it's essential to understand the importance of time management and goal setting. Time management is the process of organizing and planning how to divide your time between specific activities. Effective time management enables you to work smarter, not harder, so you get more done in less time, even when time is tight, and pressures are high.

Goal setting involves identifying what you want to achieve and establishing measurable objectives and timeframes. Goals give you direction and a sense of purpose, making it easier to focus your efforts and make decisions aligned with your priorities.

The journey from procrastination to effective time management is not easy, but it is possible with the right strategies and mindset. Mindfulness offers a powerful tool to help procrastinators break free from their habits, enabling them to manage their time more effectively and achieve their goals with less stress and greater satisfaction.

Mindful goal setting can provide a way forward. Mindfulness encourages you to stay present, acknowledge your thoughts without judgment, and gently guide your focus back to what truly matters. By practicing mindfulness, you can learn to set goals with greater clarity and intention, free from the paralyzing grip of overthinking.

Time, goals, and mindfulness form an intricate triad that influences our daily lives. Time is the finite resource we must steward wisely, goals are the milestones that give direction to our journey, and mindfulness is the anchor that keeps us present and focused amidst distractions.

Procrastination and overthinking disrupt this equilibrium, leading to inefficiency, stress, and unfulfilled ambitions. By embracing mindfulness as a core principle in our approach to time management and goal setting, we unlock the power to navigate challenges with resilience and intentionality.

The Power of Mindful Time Management

We often find ourselves overwhelmed by endless to-do lists and constant distractions. Enter mindful time management—a transformative approach that combines traditional time management techniques with the principles of mindfulness.

By focusing on the present moment, acknowledging our priorities, and embracing flexibility, we can navigate our schedules with clarity and intention.

Mindfulness invites us to fully engage with the present moment, acknowledging its significance in shaping our future. When we dwell too much on past mistakes or worry excessively about the future, we lose sight of the opportunities and tasks at hand. Practice mindfulness by grounding yourself in the here and now, appreciating each moment as a chance to make progress towards your goals.

Start your day with a brief mindfulness exercise, such as mindful breathing or a short body scan, to center yourself before diving into tasks.

Procrastination and overthinking thrive in an environment of distraction and mental clutter. Mindful time management involves cultivating focus and clarity by prioritizing tasks, setting boundaries, and minimizing distractions. When you approach each task with mindfulness, you bring heightened awareness and attention, leading to greater efficiency and quality of work.

Use the Pomodoro Technique—work for 25 minutes with full focus, then take a 5-minute break—to maintain productivity while avoiding burnout.

Pomodoro Technique Steps:

1. Choose a task you want to work on.
2. Set a timer for 25 minutes and work on the task without interruptions.
3. When the timer goes off, take a 5-minute break. Stretch, breathe, or enjoy a quick walk.

4. Repeat the process, and after four Pomodoros, take a longer break (15-30 minutes).

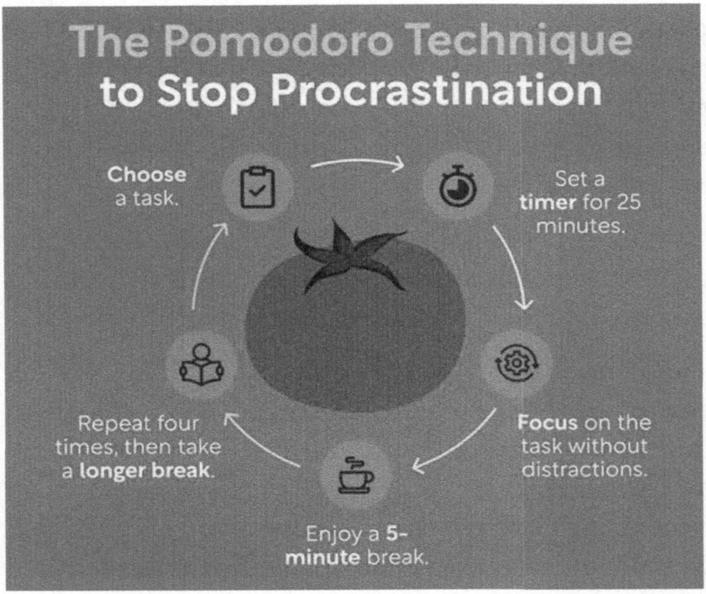

Mindfulness teaches us to embrace impermanence and adapt to changing circumstances. Effective time management requires a balance between structured planning and flexibility. Stay mindful of your goals and priorities, but remain open to adjustments and new opportunities that may arise along the way. Being rigid can lead to stress and frustration, while mindfulness fosters resilience and adaptability.

At the end of each day, review your accomplishments and adjust your plans for the next day based on insights gained.

Daily Review Steps:

1. Reflect on what you accomplished today. Celebrate small wins.
2. Identify any tasks that were left unfinished and consider why.
3. Adjust your schedule for the next day based on these reflections.
4. Set intentions for tomorrow with a positive, adaptable mindset.

Identify and prioritize tasks based on their importance and urgency. Mindfulness helps you discern between essential tasks that align with your goals and distractions that derail your progress. Prioritize mindfully by focusing on high-impact activities that move you closer to your objectives.

Use the Eisenhower Matrix (urgent vs. important) to categorize tasks and prioritize effectively.

Eisenhower Matrix Steps:

1. **Urgent and Important:** Handle these tasks immediately.
2. **Important but Not Urgent:** Schedule time to work on these tasks.
3. **Urgent but Not Important:** Delegate these tasks if possible.
4. **Not Urgent and Not Important:** Minimize or eliminate these tasks.

The Eisenhower decision matrix

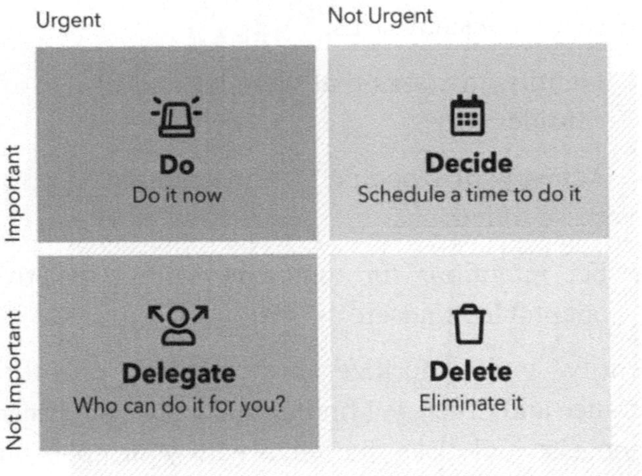

Mindfulness encourages a realistic and balanced approach to scheduling. Avoid overloading your schedule or succumbing to the temptation of multitasking, as these can lead to stress and reduced productivity. Create a realistic schedule that allows for focused work, breaks, and self-care activities.

Allocate time blocks for specific tasks, and include buffer time for unexpected interruptions or delays.

- **Daily Planner:** Use a daily planner to organize your tasks into time blocks. Be realistic about how long each task will take and leave some buffer time.

- **Single-Task Focus:** Commit to focusing on one task at a time during each time block to maximize efficiency and quality of work.

Mindfulness involves minimizing external and internal distractions that hinder productivity. Create a conducive environment for focused work by reducing clutter, setting boundaries around distractions like social media or notifications, and cultivating a mindful attitude towards interruptions.

Establish a distraction-free workspace and use mindfulness techniques to stay focused.

- **Workspace Setup:** Arrange your workspace to minimize visual and auditory distractions. Keep it clean and organized.
- **Digital Detox:** Turn off non-essential notifications and set specific times to check emails and social media.
- **Mindful Interruptions:** When distractions occur, acknowledge them mindfully and gently bring your focus back to the task at hand.

Setting SMART Goals with Mindfulness

Goals are the milestones that guide our journey towards personal and professional success. However, setting goals that are too vague or overly ambitious can lead to frustration and procrastination. This is where the concept of SMART goals—Specific, Measurable, Achievable, Relevant, and Time-bound—comes into play. How do you effectively set SMART goals? Let's understand it better.

Setting Your SMART Goals

1. **Specific**: What exactly do you want to achieve? Be clear and precise.
2. **Measurable**: How will you know when you've achieved it? Define what success looks like.
3. **Achievable**: Is this goal realistic? Consider your current commitments and resources.
4. **Relevant**: Why is this goal important to you? Ensure it aligns with your values and long-term objectives.
5. **Time-bound**: When do you want to achieve this goal? Set a deadline to keep yourself accountable.

Example:

- **Specific**: I want to complete my research paper.
- **Measurable**: I will write 500 words per day.
- **Achievable**: I will allocate 2 hours each evening.
- **Relevant**: This paper is crucial for my degree.
- **Time-bound**: I will finish by the end of the month.

When combined with mindfulness, SMART goal setting becomes even more powerful. Mindfulness helps us clarify our true aspirations, align our goals with our values, and remain focused on the steps needed to achieve them.

Use mindfulness techniques such as visualization and reflective journaling to clarify your goals and identify actionable steps.

- **Visualization:** Spend a few minutes each day visualizing your goals as if they are already achieved. Notice the details and emotions associated with this success.
- **Reflective Journaling:** Write down your goals and the specific steps needed to achieve them. Reflect on how each step aligns with your values and aspirations.

Mindfulness encourages a non-judgmental awareness of your progress. Instead of fixating on perfection or comparing yourself to others, focus on your journey and celebrate small victories along the way. Measure progress mindfully by setting milestones and regularly reflecting on your achievements.

Create a progress tracker or journal where you can record milestones, challenges overcome, and lessons learned.

- **Progress Tracker:** Use a notebook or digital tool to log your daily or weekly achievements. Note any obstacles faced and how you overcame them.

- **Milestone Celebrations:** Acknowledge and reward yourself for reaching significant milestones. This could be a small treat, a day off, or simply taking time to reflect on your progress.

Setting daily intentions aligns your actions with your long-term goals. Begin each day with a clear intention that reflects your priorities and values. This mindful practice can help you stay focused and purpose-driven throughout the day.

Start each day by setting a clear, positive intention that aligns with your goals.

- **Daily Intention Setting:** Each morning, write down your intention for the day. For example, "Today, I will focus on completing my project report with attention to detail."
- **Reflect on Intentions:** At the end of the day, reflect on how well you honored your intention and what adjustments you might make for the next day.

Mindfulness promotes a realistic and balanced approach to goal setting. Avoid setting goals that are too ambitious or unrealistic, as they can lead to frustration and demotivation. Set achievable goals that stretch your capabilities while remaining within reach with focused effort.

Break larger goals into smaller, manageable tasks to maintain momentum and track progress effectively.

- **Task Breakdown:** Divide your main goal into smaller tasks. For example, if your goal is to write a book, break it down into writing one chapter a week, then further into daily word counts.
- **Daily Task List:** Create a daily to-do list with manageable tasks that contribute to your larger goals. This helps maintain a sense of accomplishment and progress.

Mindfulness helps you align your goals with your values, passions, and long-term aspirations. Reflect on whether your goals align with your core values and contribute to your overall well-being and fulfillment. Goals that resonate with your inner purpose are more likely to inspire sustained motivation and dedication.

Regularly reassess your goals to ensure they remain relevant and meaningful in the context of your evolving priorities and aspirations.

- **Value Alignment Check:** Periodically review your goals to ensure they align with your core values. Ask yourself if the goal still excites and motivates you.
- **Adapt Goals:** Be open to adjusting your goals based on new insights and changing circumstances. This flexibility ensures continued relevance and motivation.

Mindfulness instills a sense of urgency and commitment to timelines. Set clear deadlines for each goal or milestone, keeping in mind the importance of balance and self-care. Mindful time management involves honoring your commitments while maintaining a healthy work-life balance.

Use time-blocking techniques to allocate dedicated time slots for specific tasks and ensure progress towards your goals.

- **Time-Blocking:** Schedule specific blocks of time for focused work on your goals. For example, dedicate 9-11 AM for project work without interruptions.
- **Balance with Self-Care:** Ensure your schedule includes time for self-care activities like exercise, hobbies, and relaxation to prevent burnout and **maintain overall well-being.**

Mindfulness and gratitude go hand in hand. Regularly practicing gratitude can shift your focus from what's lacking to what you have, fostering a positive mindset that supports goal achievement. Gratitude helps you appreciate the progress you've made and the resources you have.

Keep a gratitude journal and write down three things you're grateful for each day.

- **Gratitude Journal**: Each evening, write down three things you are grateful for. Reflect on how these positive aspects contribute to your overall goals and well-being.

- **Gratitude Pause**: Throughout the day, take brief moments to pause and acknowledge something you're grateful for. This practice can enhance your mood and motivation.

Being good at time management and goal setting is not just about productivity; they are also about enhancing quality of life. They allow us to make time for self-care, hobbies, and relationships, which are essential for mental and emotional health. When we feel in control of our time and have clear goals to strive towards, we experience higher levels of satisfaction and well-being.

These skills help us navigate the complexities of modern life, achieve our aspirations, and maintain a balanced and fulfilling lifestyle. For procrastinators and overthinkers, mastering these skills can transform their approach to daily tasks and long-term ambitions, paving the way for success and personal growth.

Resources

Podcasts:

1. **The Mindful Kind** – Practical advice and tips on mindfulness.
2. **10% Happier** – Interviews and insights on mindfulness and meditation.
3. **On Being** – Conversations exploring the human experience and mindful living

Key Takeaways

- Time management and goal setting are essential for balancing productivity, well-being, and fulfillment in both personal and professional life.
- Effective time management involves prioritizing tasks, setting boundaries, and reducing distractions, creating a sense of control and reducing stress.
- Clear, achievable goals provide direction and motivation, helping focus efforts on meaningful activities and avoid wasting time on distractions.
- Procrastination, often fueled by underestimating time needs and prioritizing easier tasks, disrupts productivity and increases stress.

- Overthinking hinders decision-making through perfectionism, fear of failure, and magnifying obstacles, leading to delays and inefficiency.
- Mindfulness supports time management and goal setting by fostering present-moment awareness, reducing distractions, and encouraging intentional action.
- Strategies like SMART goals, time-blocking, the Eisenhower Matrix, and the Pomodoro Technique enhance focus and efficiency.
- Regular reflection, gratitude practices, and aligning goals with personal values promote sustainable motivation and a balanced lifestyle.
- Embracing mindfulness and realistic planning transforms procrastination and overthinking into progress and achievement.

Chapter 5

Overcoming Perfectionism

When you have a big project to tackle—a presentation for work or a paper for school— do you often find yourself wanting it to be perfect? So, you spend hours researching, planning, and refining every detail in your mind. You want every slide, every word, every idea to be flawless. But as the deadline looms closer, you find yourself hesitating. Doubts start creeping in. What if it's not good enough? What if you make a mistake? What if others criticize your work?

This is where perfectionism steps in and becomes a silent saboteur. It convinces you that unless everything is perfect, it's not worth starting at all. You tell yourself you need more time to get it just right, so you delay starting the project. This delay is procrastination's playground, and perfectionism is the gatekeeper keeping you from taking that first step.

Procrastination feeds on perfectionism's desire for flawlessness. It whispers that you need more information, more preparation, more time to make everything perfect. It convinces you that starting now would be a mistake because you might not have all the answers or all the skills yet. So, you put it off for later, hoping that somehow, magically, everything will fall into place when you finally start.

Perfectionism can have profound effects on productivity, often leading to a paradoxical decrease in overall output despite high levels of effort.

Research conducted by Dr. Gordon L. Flett and Dr. Paul L. Hewitt (1991) sheds light on the relationship between perfectionism and procrastination, highlighting how perfectionists tend to delay tasks due to the fear of not meeting their own lofty standards. This procrastination, fueled by the perfectionistic mindset, ultimately results in lower productivity levels.

Furthermore, the pursuit of perfection can lead to excessive time spent on tasks. A study by Stoeber and Otto (2006) found that perfectionists often engage in over-preparation, spending more time than necessary on a task in an attempt to ensure perfection.

This tendency to perfectionistic overkill can lead to diminishing returns, where the additional time invested does not proportionally increase the quality of the outcome. As a result, perfectionists may find themselves mired in details and unable to complete tasks efficiently.

Often in the professional sphere, perfectionists may struggle with delegation and collaboration. A study published in the Journal of Vocational Behavior (Hill et al., 2010) explored the impact of perfectionism on teamwork, revealing that perfectionists may have difficulty trusting others to meet their high standards. This reluctance to delegate tasks or collaborate effectively can hinder productivity, as it limits the sharing of workload and expertise.

Perfectionism and procrastination are a deceptive duo. The more you delay, the more pressure you feel to meet those sky-high standards of perfection you've set for yourself. And as the pressure mounts, so does the fear of failure. What if you can't meet those impossible standards? What if your work doesn't measure up to your own expectations?

This fear of falling short fuels overthinking. You start second-guessing every decision, every idea. You analyze and re-analyze, trying to anticipate every possible outcome, every potential flaw. But the more you think, the more overwhelming it becomes. The task seems insurmountable, and you feel paralyzed by the weight of perfectionism's demands.

Overthinking becomes a trap—a never-ending cycle of analysis and doubt. You get stuck in a loop of indecision, unable to move forward because you're too busy overthinking every detail. Every choice feels monumental, every step feels risky. And so, you stay stuck, unable to break free from perfectionism's grip.

Analysis-paralysis is a common phenomenon associated with perfectionism, characterized by excessive overthinking and indecision. Perfectionists tend to get caught in a loop of analyzing every possible option, outcome, and consequence, leading to a state of cognitive overload and inaction.

The concept of analysis-paralysis is supported by research in decision-making psychology. A study by Schwartz et al. (2002) explored the impact of choice overload on decision-making, revealing that an abundance of options can lead to increased anxiety and difficulty making decisions. Perfectionists, who often seek the "perfect" choice, are particularly susceptible to this overload, as they strive to evaluate every possible scenario before taking action.

To overcome analysis-paralysis, individuals must learn to balance thoughtful analysis with decisive action. Setting time limits for decision-making, prioritizing options, and focusing on key criteria can help break the cycle of overthinking and facilitate progress toward goals.

Recognizing the detrimental effects of analysis-paralysis is the first step in cultivating a more effective and efficient approach to decision-making.

Perfectionism, while often associated with high standards and ambition, can also have significant effects on well-being. Research by Dr. Randy Frost and colleagues (2013) highlights the link between perfectionism and increased levels of stress, anxiety, and depression. Perfectionists tend to experience heightened levels of self-criticism and fear of failure, leading to chronic stress and emotional strain.

Moreover, the relentless pursuit of perfection can result in burnout—a state of physical, emotional, and mental exhaustion. A study by Stoeber and Rennert (2008) found that perfectionists are more prone to burnout due to their tendency to set unrealistically high standards and engage in excessive self-criticism.

This constant pressure to meet impossible expectations can take a toll on overall well-being, leading to feelings of fatigue, irritability, and disillusionment.

Additionally, it can impact relationships and social interactions. Research published in the Journal of Personality and Social Psychology (Hewitt et al., 2006) suggests that perfectionists may struggle with interpersonal relationships, as their rigid standards and critical self-evaluations can create barriers to intimacy and connection. This social isolation and fear of judgment can further contribute to feelings of loneliness and emotional distress.

Addressing and overcoming perfectionism requires a compassionate and growth-oriented mindset. It's essential to approach this journey with self-awareness, self-compassion, and a willingness to embrace imperfection as part of the learning process.

By shifting our perspective from perfection to progress, we open ourselves up to new possibilities and opportunities for growth. The journey to overcoming perfectionism is not about achieving flawlessness but about embracing our humanity, celebrating our efforts, and learning from our mistakes. It's a journey of self-discovery, resilience, and personal development.

So, how can you challenge your perfectionist thinking? Here are some suggestions that can help you break free from the constraints of perfectionism, encouraging growth, resilience, and a more balanced approach to life.

Set Realistic Standards: Perfectionists often set impossibly high standards for themselves, leading to constant feelings of inadequacy. Start by identifying these unrealistic standards and questioning their necessity.

Ask yourself if achieving perfection is truly essential or if striving for progress and improvement is a more realistic and fulfilling goal. Focus on setting specific, achievable goals that align with your values and priorities.

Practice Self-Compassion: Perfectionists are often their own harshest critics, leading to a cycle of self-criticism and low self-esteem. Cultivate self-compassion by treating yourself with the same kindness and understanding you would offer to a friend facing a similar challenge.

Use self-compassionate language and affirmations, acknowledging that mistakes and setbacks are part of the learning process and do not define your worth.

Reframe Mistakes as Learning Opportunities: Instead of viewing mistakes as failures, reframe them as valuable learning experiences. Adopt a growth mindset, recognizing that challenges and setbacks provide opportunities for growth and improvement.

Reflect on what you can learn from each experience and how you can apply those lessons moving forward. Embrace the idea that progress is made through trial and error, not perfection.

Set Time Limits for Decisions: Analysis-paralysis often stems from overthinking and indecision. Combat this by setting time limits for decision-making.

Give yourself a specific window of time to gather information, weigh options, and make a decision. Trust your instincts and accept that not every decision will be perfect, but taking action is better than endless deliberation.

Challenge All-or-Nothing Thinking: Perfectionists tend to think in black-and-white terms, believing that something is either perfect or a failure. Challenge this mindset by embracing the gray areas. Recognize that perfection is an unrealistic standard and that progress is made through incremental improvements. Celebrate small victories and acknowledge that every step forward, no matter how small, is meaningful.

Focus on Progress, Not Perfection: Shift your focus from achieving perfection to making progress. Set realistic goals and celebrate milestones along the way.

Break large tasks into smaller, manageable steps, allowing yourself to make steady progress without the pressure of perfection. Acknowledge and appreciate the effort you put into each task, regardless of the outcome.

Practice Mindfulness and Acceptance: Mindfulness involves being present in the moment and accepting things as they are, without judgment. Practice mindfulness techniques such as deep breathing, meditation, or mindful awareness of thoughts and emotions. Cultivate acceptance of yourself and your circumstances, letting go of the need for constant control and perfection.

Seek Support and Feedback: Don't be afraid to reach out for support from trusted friends, mentors, or therapists. Share your goals, challenges, and progress with others who can offer constructive feedback and guidance.

Collaborate with others and be open to learning from different perspectives. Constructive feedback can help you gain valuable insights and navigate perfectionistic tendencies more effectively.

Tangible exercises play a crucial role in holding yourself accountable when it comes to overcoming perfectionism. Unlike abstract concepts or vague goals, tangible exercises provide actionable steps and measurable progress markers. They serve as concrete tools to implement change, track your efforts, and hold yourself accountable to your growth journey.

By engaging in specific exercises, you create a framework for taking consistent action, confronting perfectionist tendencies, and fostering a healthier mindset. These exercises act as checkpoints along the way, helping you stay focused, motivated, and accountable to the process of embracing imperfection. Let's delve deeper into some of these tangible exercises.

Progress Journaling: Begin by setting up a progress journal—a dedicated space where you can track your journey towards overcoming perfectionism. In this journal, you'll record not just the end results of your efforts but also the steps you took along the way.

It's a place to celebrate small victories, acknowledge challenges overcome, and reflect on the growth that comes from embracing imperfection.

Imperfect Practice: Embracing imperfection starts with intentional practice. Choose an activity or skill that you enjoy but often shy away from due to perfectionist tendencies. This could be anything from painting to playing a musical instrument or even trying a new sport.

The key is to approach this practice session with the mindset of allowing mistakes and learning from them, rather than striving for flawless performance.

Time-Limited Tasks: Time-limited tasks are a practical way to challenge perfectionism's grip on your productivity. Set specific time limits for completing tasks or segments of a project. For example, if you have a report to write, allocate a set amount of time for research, drafting, and editing, and stick to those time frames. This exercise encourages you to focus on progress and completion rather than perfection.

Permission Slips: Write yourself permission slips as a symbolic gesture of letting go of perfectionist expectations. These slips serve as reminders that it's okay to make mistakes, try new things, and learn along the way. Keep them visible in your workspace as gentle prompts to embrace imperfection and self-compassion.

Feedback Sessions: Feedback is a powerful tool for growth, especially when overcoming perfectionism. Initiate regular feedback sessions with trusted colleagues, mentors, or friends. Create a safe space for constructive criticism and focus on learning from feedback rather than viewing it as a judgment of your worth. These sessions foster a growth mindset and resilience in the face of imperfection.

Mindful Breathing Exercises: Incorporating mindfulness into your routine can significantly reduce perfectionist tendencies and anxiety. Start with simple mindful breathing exercises.

Find a quiet space, sit comfortably, and focus on your breath. Notice the sensations of each inhale and exhale, allowing thoughts to come and go without judgment. This practice cultivates a sense of calm and presence, reducing the urge to seek perfection.

Visualization Techniques: Visualization is a powerful tool for reprogramming perfectionist thinking patterns. Begin by visualizing yourself successfully completing a task or project without everything being perfect.

Imagine the journey—the challenges faced, the mistakes made, and the lessons learned. Visualize the satisfaction and pride you feel in your progress and effort, shifting the focus from flawless results to meaningful growth.

Challenge Perfectionist Language: Pay attention to the language you use when talking to yourself. Notice any perfectionist phrases like "I must," "I should," or "It has to be perfect." Challenge these thoughts by replacing them with more flexible and compassionate language. For example, replace "It has to be perfect" with "I'll do my best and learn from the outcome."

Experiment with Imperfect Solutions: Purposefully seek out opportunities to implement imperfect solutions or approaches.

Instead of spending excessive time trying to find the perfect solution, choose a good enough option and assess its effectiveness. Embracing imperfection in problem-solving can lead to quicker decision-making and innovation.

Celebrate Mistakes and Failures: Shift your perspective on mistakes and failures by celebrating them as valuable learning experiences.

Create a "failure celebration" ritual where you acknowledge and learn from mistakes rather than dwelling on them. Share your failures with others, reflect on the lessons learned, and appreciate the growth that comes from embracing imperfection.

Embracing imperfection is a courageous journey towards self-acceptance and genuine growth. In a world that often values flawless performance and unyielding standards, challenging perfectionist thinking is a radical act of self-compassion and resilience. By incorporating these practical exercises into your daily routine, you can cultivate a healthier mindset that values progress over perfection.

Recognise and Overcome Your Perfectionist Tendencies

Identify Perfectionist Tendencies: Reflect on the following questions and jot down your thoughts:

- Do you often procrastinate because you're afraid of making mistakes?
- Do you feel that your work is never good enough?
- Are you overly critical of yourself and others?
- Do you avoid tasks or projects if you can't do them perfectly?

Rate Your Perfectionism: On a scale of 1 to 10, rate how much perfectionism impacts various areas of your life:

- Work/School
- Personal Projects
- Relationships
- Self-Care

Challenge Negative Thoughts: Identify a recent perfectionist thought and reframe it. Example:

- **Negative Thought:** "If it's not perfect, it's a failure."
- **Reframed Thought:** "Doing my best is what matters, and I can learn from any mistakes."

Affirmations: Write down three affirmations to counter perfectionist tendencies. Example:

- "I am proud of my progress."
- "Mistakes are opportunities for growth."
- "I am enough just as I am."

Weekly Reflection: At the end of each week, review your progress. What steps did you take towards your goals? What did you learn from any mistakes? Celebrate your achievements and note areas for improvement.

Monthly Check-In: Each month, assess how your perfectionism has changed. Have you become more accepting of imperfection? Are you more productive and less stressed? Adjust your goals and strategies as needed.

Resources

Books:

- "The Gifts of Imperfection" by Brené Brown
- "Mindset: The New Psychology of Success" by Carol S. Dweck
- "Radical Acceptance" by Tara Brach

Podcasts:

- "The One You Feed" by Eric Zimmer and Chris Forbes: Explores how mindfulness and self-compassion can improve mental well-being.
- "Unlocking Us" by Brené Brown: Covers topics related to vulnerability, courage, and imperfection.

Key Takeaways

- Perfectionism often leads to procrastination, as the desire for flawlessness can create fear of failure and hesitation to start tasks.
- Overthinking and analysis-paralysis are common among perfectionists, causing delays and cognitive overload.
- Perfectionism negatively impacts productivity, collaboration, and well-being, often resulting in burnout, stress, and emotional strain.

- Research highlights the link between perfectionism and increased anxiety, depression, and challenges in relationships.
- Shifting focus from perfection to progress, practicing self-compassion, and reframing mistakes as learning opportunities can help overcome perfectionism.
- Practical strategies like time-limited tasks, feedback sessions, progress journaling, and mindfulness exercises encourage growth and resilience.
- Celebrating small achievements and adopting affirmations can foster a healthier mindset and reduce the grip of perfectionism.
- Embracing imperfection allows for greater productivity, self-acceptance, and meaningful personal development.

Chapter 6

Cultivating Self-Compassion

The practice of treating oneself with kindness and understanding during times of failure or difficulty, also known as self-compassion, is a transformative approach that can significantly impact mental well-being and productivity. As Dr. Kristin Neff eloquently puts it, "With self-compassion, we give ourselves the same kindness and care we'd give to a good friend."

It's a concept that has gained significant attention in psychological research, largely due to the work of Dr. Kristin Neff, a pioneering researcher in the field. Self-compassion involves three main components: self-kindness, common humanity, and mindfulness.

Self-kindness refers to being warm and understanding toward ourselves when we suffer, fail, or feel inadequate, rather than ignoring our pain or being self-critical. It means recognizing that imperfection is part of the shared human experience.

As Dr. Neff explains, "You can't always get what you want. You can't always be who you want to be. You can't always be who you want others to think you are. When this reality is denied or resisted, suffering arises in the form of stress, frustration, and self-criticism."

Common humanity involves recognizing that suffering and personal inadequacy are part of the shared human experience – something that we all go through rather than something that happens to "me" alone. When we feel isolated by our imperfections, we amplify our suffering. By understanding that pain and failure are universal, we can foster a sense of connection and reduce feelings of isolation.

Mindfulness is the balanced approach to negative emotions so that feelings are neither suppressed nor exaggerated. Mindfulness requires that we do not "over-identify" with thoughts and feelings, so that we are not swept away by negative reactivity. As Jon Kabat-Zinn says, "Mindfulness means paying attention in a particular way: on purpose, in the present moment, and non-judgmentally."

Despite its benefits, many people find it challenging to cultivate self-compassion. Understanding the barriers to self-compassion can help us overcome them and foster a healthier relationship with ourselves. One significant reason people struggle with self-compassion is the pervasive culture of self-criticism.

From a young age, many of us are taught to push ourselves to be better and to strive for perfection. While striving for improvement isn't inherently negative, it often comes with an underlying message: "You're not good enough as you are." Dr. Kristin Neff explains, "Our culture teaches us that being hard on ourselves is the way to be." This ingrained habit of self-criticism makes it difficult to switch to a mindset of self-kindness.

Perfectionism is another barrier to self-compassion. Many people hold themselves to impossibly high standards and feel intense self-criticism when they fail to meet these standards. Perfectionism can create a fear of failure that prevents individuals from being kind to themselves.

A study by Dr. Paul Hewitt and Dr. Gordon Flett found that perfectionism is associated with increased levels of anxiety, depression, and low self-esteem. This toxic cycle makes it hard for individuals to adopt a compassionate attitude towards themselves.

The fear of self-indulgence also plays a role in why people resist self-compassion. Many believe that being kind to oneself is synonymous with being lazy or self-indulgent. This misconception is fueled by the idea that self-criticism is necessary for motivation and success.

However, research by Dr. Kristin Neff and Dr. Roos Vonk indicates that self-compassionate individuals are more likely to take responsibility for their actions and make positive changes. Neff clarifies, "Self-compassion is not about letting yourself off the hook; it's about recognizing your mistakes and learning from them."

Social comparison exacerbates the difficulty of practicing self-compassion. In the age of social media, where people often present idealized versions of their lives, it's easy to fall into the trap of comparing oneself to others.

This constant comparison can lead to feelings of inadequacy and self-criticism. Dr. Neff's research shows that self-compassion is linked to lower levels of social comparison and envy. By focusing on our own journey and treating ourselves with kindness, we can mitigate the negative effects of social comparison.

Another factor is the fear of vulnerability. Many people equate self-compassion with weakness, believing that acknowledging their suffering or failures makes them vulnerable. This fear is often rooted in societal norms that value stoicism and self-reliance.

However, research by Dr. Brené Brown, a professor at the University of Houston, emphasizes that vulnerability is essential for emotional well-being. Brown states, "Vulnerability is the birthplace of love, belonging, joy, courage, empathy, and creativity." Embracing vulnerability through self-compassion allows us to connect more deeply with ourselves and others.

Childhood experiences also play a significant role in shaping our ability to be self-compassionate. Individuals who grew up in environments where they were criticized or their emotions were invalidated often internalize these negative messages. This internalized criticism becomes a barrier to self-compassion in adulthood. A study by Dr. Brian W. Knutson and Dr. Rebecca J. L. Shankman found that individuals who experienced harsh parenting were more likely to develop self-critical tendencies. Recognizing and addressing these ingrained patterns is crucial for developing self-compassion.

Lastly, societal stigma around mental health can deter individuals from practicing self-compassion. Many people are reluctant to acknowledge their emotional struggles due to fear of judgment or stigma. This reluctance can prevent them from treating themselves with the kindness and understanding they need.

According to a report by the World Health Organization (WHO), stigma is a major barrier to seeking help for mental health issues. By fostering a more compassionate attitude towards ourselves, we can challenge these societal stigmas and promote better mental health.

Research has shown that self-compassion is associated with greater emotional resilience, more accurate self-concepts, and more caring relationship behavior. A study by Neff and colleagues (2007) found that self-compassion provides similar benefits to self-esteem but without the pitfalls of egotism and social comparison. Additionally, self-compassion has been linked to lower levels of anxiety and depression, as well as greater overall well-being.

When it comes to procrastination, self-compassion is a powerful antidote. One of the primary reasons we procrastinate is the fear of failing. When we are self-compassionate, we can acknowledge this fear without letting it control us. Instead of berating ourselves for being afraid, we can offer ourselves words of comfort and encouragement.

Research by Breines and Chen (2012) found that self-compassionate individuals are more likely to see failure as a learning opportunity rather than a reflection of their worth, reducing the fear that fuels procrastination.

Procrastination often stems from emotional overwhelm. When faced with a daunting task, we might feel anxious or stressed, leading us to avoid the task altogether. Self-compassion helps build emotional resilience, allowing us to cope with these negative emotions more effectively.

By practicing self-kindness, we create a supportive inner environment that can withstand the ups and downs of life. This makes it easier to start and persist with challenging tasks.

Interestingly, self-compassion also boosts motivation. A study by Neff, Hsieh, and Dejitterat (2005) showed that students who practiced self-compassion were more motivated to learn and improve after receiving negative feedback, compared to those who were self-critical. This is because self-compassionate individuals are less likely to be debilitated by self-doubt and more likely to maintain a positive outlook on their ability to grow and succeed.

The habit of overthinking comes from a deep-seated fear of making mistakes, being judged, or not being good enough. It involves getting trapped in a cycle of negative thoughts and anxieties that paralyze us, making it difficult to take action or make decisions. Self-compassion can be a crucial tool in breaking free from this cycle.

When we overthink, we're lost in a maze of thoughts, many of which are negative and unproductive. Mindfulness, a key component of self-compassion, helps us become aware of these thought patterns without getting entangled in them.

By observing our thoughts non-judgmentally, we can break the cycle of rumination and focus on the present moment. This mindful approach can significantly reduce the stress and anxiety that fuel overthinking.

Self-compassion encourages us to accept our imperfections and mistakes as part of being human. When we overthink, it's usually because we're trying to control outcomes or punish ourselves for perceived failures. By embracing self-compassion, we learn to accept that not everything will go perfectly and that it's okay to make mistakes. This acceptance can liberate us from the need to overthink every decision and action.

Common humanity, another component of self-compassion, reminds us that we are not alone in our struggles. Everyone experiences difficulties and makes mistakes. This perspective can be incredibly freeing, as it helps us realize that our problems are not unique or insurmountable. By seeing our experiences as part of the broader human condition, we can reduce the self-criticism that often drives overthinking.

Cultivating self-compassion and self-acceptance is a transformative journey that can significantly enhance your mental well-being and overall quality of life. Here are some easy-to-do exercises and practices designed to help you develop these crucial skills. Each exercise is practical and intended to be integrated into your daily routine, making the path to self-compassion and self-acceptance both accessible and rewarding.

Mindful Self-Compassion Break

The Mindful Self-Compassion Break is a quick and powerful way to address immediate stress and negative self-talk. By acknowledging your suffering, recognizing it as a shared human experience, and offering yourself kindness, you can break the cycle of self-criticism and cultivate a more compassionate mindset. This exercise helps you shift from harsh self-judgment to gentle understanding, providing emotional relief in moments of distress.

How to Do It:

1. **Recognize**: When you notice you're feeling stressed or criticizing yourself, pause for a moment.
2. **Acknowledge**: Place your hand over your heart and acknowledge your feelings. Say to yourself, "This is a moment of suffering."
3. **Common Humanity**: Remind yourself that suffering is a part of life and that everyone experiences moments like this. Say, "Suffering is a part of life. I'm not alone in this."
4. **Self-Kindness**: Offer yourself kind words. Say something like, "May I be kind to myself," or "May I give myself the compassion that I need."

Self-Compassion Journal

Writing in a Self-Compassion Journal fosters a habit of self-kindness and enhances your awareness of personal struggles and strengths. By reflecting on difficult experiences, recognizing shared humanity, and offering kind messages to yourself, you build resilience and a more supportive inner dialogue. This practice encourages a balanced perspective on your challenges and promotes a positive, compassionate approach to self-reflection.

How to Do It:

1. **Daily Entry**: Each evening, spend 10-15 minutes writing in a journal.
2. **Three Sections**:
   - **Mindfulness**: Write about a difficult experience you had during the day. Describe your emotions and thoughts without judgment.
   - **Common Humanity**: Reflect on how many people might experience similar challenges. Write about this shared human experience.
   - **Self-Kindness**: Write a kind, comforting message to yourself. Imagine what you would say to a dear friend in a similar situation and write those words to yourself.

Positive Affirmations

Positive Affirmations counteract negative self-talk and build a positive self-image by reinforcing constructive beliefs about yourself. By repeating affirmations, you gradually replace self-doubt with confidence and self-acceptance. This daily practice helps to rewire your brain, making it easier to maintain a positive outlook and approach challenges with a growth mindset.

How to Do It:

1. **Identify Affirmations**: Write down a list of positive affirmations that resonate with you. Examples include "I am worthy of love and respect," "I am capable and strong," and "I accept myself as I am."
2. **Daily Practice**: Every morning, stand in front of a mirror, look into your eyes, and repeat your affirmations out loud. Do this with conviction and believe in the words you are saying.
3. **Visual Reminders**: Write your affirmations on sticky notes and place them where you can see them throughout the day (e.g., on your bathroom mirror, computer screen, or fridge).

Self-Compassionate Letter

Writing a Self-Compassionate Letter offers comfort and understanding during tough times by providing a nurturing perspective on your struggles. By expressing empathy and support in writing, you create a tangible reminder of your worth and resilience. This helps you practice self-kindness and reduces self-criticism, enabling a more compassionate and accepting attitude towards yourself.

How to Do It:

1. **Write a Letter**: Think of a situation that is causing you distress or self-criticism. Write a letter to yourself from the perspective of a compassionate friend.
2. **Express Understanding**: Acknowledge your feelings and the difficulty of the situation. Express empathy and understanding.
3. **Offer Comfort**: Provide words of comfort and support. Remind yourself of your strengths and past successes.
4. **Re-read Often**: Keep this letter and read it whenever you're feeling down or self-critical.

Self-Compassionate Breathing

Self-Compassionate Breathing creates a physical sense of comfort and relaxation, helping you manage stress and negative emotions. By focusing on your breath and imagining warmth and kindness with each inhale and exhale, you cultivate a soothing inner experience. This practice enhances your ability to stay present and calm, making it easier to face challenges with a compassionate mindset.

How to Do It:

1. **Find a Quiet Space**: Sit or lie down in a comfortable position.
2. **Focus on Breath**: Close your eyes and take a few deep, calming breaths.
3. **Place Your Hand on Your Heart**: Feel the warmth of your hand and the gentle rise and fall of your chest.
4. **Breathe with Compassion**: As you breathe in, imagine you are inhaling warmth and kindness. As you breathe out, let go of stress and tension. Repeat phrases like "I am safe" or "I am loved" with each breath.

Engage in Creative Activities

Engaging in creative activities allows you to express yourself and build self-acceptance through artistic outlets. By doing these activities like painting, writing, or playing music, you focus on the creative process rather than the outcome. This practice encourages experimentation and self-discovery, promoting a sense of joy and acceptance as you explore your creative potential.

How to Do It:

1. **Choose a Creative Activity**: Pick an activity that you enjoy or have always wanted to try (painting, drawing, writing, dancing, playing music).
2. **Set Aside Time**: Dedicate regular time each week to engage in this activity.
3. **Focus on the Process**: Rather than focusing on the outcome, immerse yourself in the creative process. Allow yourself to experiment and make mistakes.
4. **Reflect on Your Experience**: After each session, take a few moments to reflect on how the activity made you feel and what you learned about yourself.

We've explored the essence of self-compassion, delved into the barriers that make it challenging, and examined practical exercises to nurture this vital skill. Embracing self-compassion is not a one-time event; it is a continuous, transformative practice that has the power to profoundly impact our lives.

Imagine waking up each day with a sense of inner peace, knowing that you are your own best ally. Picture navigating life's inevitable ups and downs with a gentle, forgiving heart. This is the promise of self-compassion.

By treating ourselves with the same kindness and understanding that we offer to others, we create a nurturing environment for growth and healing. We learn to see our imperfections not as failures but as part of our shared humanity, fostering a deeper connection with ourselves and those around us.

Remember, the barriers to self-compassion are not insurmountable. They are challenges that many of us face, but with awareness and practice, they can be overcome. Acknowledge these barriers without judgment, and use them as stepping stones towards greater self-understanding and acceptance.

The exercises we have explored are tools to help cultivate this mindset. They are practices that can be integrated into our daily routines, gradually reshaping our inner dialogue. Start small, and be patient with yourself. Change takes time, but every step forward is a victory.

As you continue your journey, remember that self-compassion is not about being perfect or always getting it right. It's about embracing your humanness and being gentle with yourself, especially in moments of struggle. It's about recognizing that you are worthy of love and kindness, not because of what you do, but simply because you are.

In this fast-paced, often harsh world, self-compassion is a radical act of self-care and resilience. It empowers us to face our fears, heal our wounds, and live more authentically. So, let us commit to being our own best friends, celebrating our successes, and comforting ourselves in our failures. Let us practice self-compassion with the same dedication we would extend to nurturing any other meaningful relationship in our lives. In doing so, we not only transform our relationship with ourselves but also radiate kindness and understanding to the world around us.

Key Takeaways

- Self-compassion, as defined by Dr. Kristin Neff, involves treating oneself with kindness, recognizing shared humanity, and practicing mindfulness during times of failure or difficulty.
- The three components of self-compassion—self-kindness, common humanity, and mindfulness—help reduce self-criticism, foster emotional resilience, and promote a balanced perspective on challenges.
- Barriers to self-compassion include cultural emphasis on self-criticism, perfectionism, fear of self-indulgence, social comparison, fear of vulnerability, harsh childhood experiences, and mental health stigma.
- Research links self-compassion to reduced anxiety, depression, and procrastination, while enhancing motivation, emotional resilience, and overall well-being.
- Self-compassion helps counter procrastination and overthinking by reframing failure as a learning opportunity, breaking cycles of negative thoughts, and fostering acceptance of imperfections.

- Practical exercises such as self-compassion journaling, mindful breathing, writing compassionate letters, and positive affirmations cultivate self-kindness and emotional growth.
- Engaging in creative activities encourages self-acceptance by focusing on the process rather than the outcome, promoting joy and experimentation.
- Self-compassion is a continuous practice that fosters inner peace, resilience, and authentic living, transforming our relationship with ourselves and others.

Chapter 7

Building Resilience

Life is full of ups and downs, and resilience is the skill that helps us bounce back from setbacks. A student facing a series of tough exams, a professional dealing with a demanding project, or a parent juggling work and family responsibilities – in these scenarios, resilience is the ability to recover from stress, adapt to change, and keep moving forward.

Take the student, for example. Despite failing a test, they decide to study harder, seek help from a tutor, and eventually improve their grades. This is resilience in action.

For the professional, resilience might mean staying calm under pressure, finding creative solutions to problems, and maintaining a positive attitude, even when deadlines loom. And for the parent, resilience is about managing the chaos of daily life, finding balance, and staying hopeful during tough times.

Resilience is not just about big challenges. It's also about handling everyday stressors, like dealing with traffic, managing a busy schedule, or facing minor disappointments. By building resilience, we become better equipped to handle whatever life throws our way, making it easier to navigate both major life events and daily hassles.

Resilience is often defined as the ability to recover from setbacks, adapt well to change, and keep going in the face of adversity. According to the American Psychological Association, resilience involves behaviors, thoughts, and actions that can be learned and developed in anyone.

Research by psychologists like Ann Masten describes resilience as "ordinary magic," highlighting that it's a common trait we all have the potential to cultivate. Masten's work emphasizes that resilience is not an extraordinary ability but a normal process of human adaptation.

Further studies by George Bonanno on resilience in trauma survivors show that resilience is a prevalent and natural response. His research indicates that most people demonstrate resilience after traumatic events, which challenges the notion that only a few individuals possess this trait.

Research in psychology and neuroscience has shed light on how resilience works. The brain's ability to adapt and reorganize itself, known as neuroplasticity, plays a significant role. Positive experiences and practices such as mindfulness and gratitude can enhance neural pathways associated with resilience.

A study conducted by Dr. Richard Davidson, a neuroscientist at the University of Wisconsin-Madison, found that mindfulness meditation can increase activity in the prefrontal cortex, the part of the brain responsible for planning, decision-making, and emotional regulation. This increased activity helps individuals manage stress more effectively and improves their ability to recover from setbacks.

The concept of resilience also includes factors like emotional regulation, social support, and a sense of purpose. These elements help individuals manage stress and bounce back from challenges. Studies have shown that people with strong social networks and a clear sense of purpose are more resilient, highlighting the importance of community and meaningful goals in building resilience.

Resilience plays a crucial role in our daily lives by helping us manage stress, stay focused, and maintain a positive outlook. When we encounter challenges, whether big or small, resilience allows us to respond effectively rather than being overwhelmed.

In the workplace, resilience helps us cope with pressure, adapt to changes, and maintain productivity. Employees who are resilient are better able to handle criticism, stay motivated, and collaborate with colleagues, leading to a more harmonious and efficient work environment.

At home, resilience helps us deal with family conflicts, financial pressures, and other personal challenges. It enables us to stay calm, communicate effectively, and find solutions to problems. Resilient individuals are also better at balancing their personal and professional lives, reducing the risk of burnout.

In social settings, resilience allows us to maintain healthy relationships and support others. When we face misunderstandings or conflicts with friends, resilience helps us navigate these situations with empathy and patience. It also enables us to provide support to others, creating a network of mutual assistance and understanding.

Furthermore, resilience contributes to overall well-being. It promotes mental and emotional health by reducing the impact of stress and preventing negative emotions from taking over. Resilient people are more likely to engage in healthy behaviors, such as regular exercise and maintaining a balanced diet, which further enhances their ability to cope with stress.

Resilience can be a powerful tool in overcoming procrastination and overthinking, two common obstacles that hinder productivity and well-being. By fostering a resilient mindset, we can develop strategies to tackle these issues effectively.

When it comes to procrastination, resilience helps us build the confidence and determination needed to start and complete tasks, even when they seem daunting. A resilient person views challenges as opportunities for growth rather than threats, making it easier to take the first step and stay committed.

For instance, when faced with a large project, a resilient individual might break it down into smaller, manageable tasks and set realistic goals. This approach reduces the feeling of being overwhelmed and makes it easier to make steady progress. Additionally, resilience helps us develop self-discipline and time management skills, which are essential in combating procrastination.

Overthinking can often lead to anxiety and indecision. Resilience equips us with the ability to regulate our emotions and maintain a balanced perspective. This means we can recognize when we're overthinking and take steps to refocus our thoughts on constructive actions.

Mindfulness practices, a component of resilience, can be particularly effective in reducing overthinking. By staying present and focusing on the here and now, we can prevent our minds from spiraling into negative thought patterns. Resilience also encourages us to seek feedback and support from others, helping us gain different perspectives and solutions to our concerns.

Taking active steps to build resilience is essential because it equips us to handle life's inevitable challenges more effectively. Resilience is not an inherent trait that some people are born with while others are not; rather, it is a skill that can be developed over time through intentional practice and effort. Here are a few reasons why actively building resilience is important:

1. **Enhances Mental Health**: Resilience helps protect against mental health issues such as anxiety, depression, and stress-related disorders. By developing resilience, individuals can better manage their emotions and maintain a sense of balance, even during difficult times.

2. **Improves Adaptability**: Life is unpredictable, and changes can occur suddenly and without warning. Resilience enhances our ability to adapt to new situations, whether they involve personal relationships, work, or health. This adaptability is crucial for maintaining stability and continuing to thrive in the face of change.

3. **Boosts Confidence and Self-Esteem**: Resilient individuals are more likely to view challenges as opportunities for growth rather than insurmountable obstacles. This positive outlook builds confidence and self-esteem, empowering individuals to take on new challenges and pursue their goals with determination.

4. **Fosters Stronger Relationships**: Resilience helps individuals communicate more effectively, manage conflicts, and provide support to others. These skills are essential for building and maintaining strong, healthy relationships with family, friends, and colleagues.

5. **Enhances Problem-Solving Skills**: Resilience involves the ability to think critically and creatively when faced with challenges. This improved problem-solving capability not only helps in overcoming obstacles but also contributes to personal and professional growth.

Just like physical strength is built through regular exercise, resilience is developed through consistent practice and intentional effort. Building resilience is a holistic process that encompasses mental, emotional, and physical well-being. It requires us to address all aspects of our lives and strive for balance.

By nurturing our minds, our emotions through mindfulness and self-compassion, and our bodies through healthy habits, we create a strong, interconnected foundation for resilience.

The following strategies offer practical exercises and tips to help you cultivate resilience and maintain a positive outlook, even in the face of adversity. By integrating these practices into your daily routine, you can strengthen your mental and emotional fortitude, enabling you to bounce back from setbacks, adapt to change, and thrive in all aspects of life.

Whether you're dealing with minor stressors or significant life challenges, these strategies will provide you with the tools needed to foster resilience and achieve a sense of balance and well-being.

Cultivate a Positive Mindset

A positive mindset is the foundation of resilience. It involves seeing challenges as opportunities, maintaining hope, and focusing on solutions rather than problems. Life is inherently unpredictable, and attempting to control every aspect can lead to frustration and anxiety. Instead, focus on what you can control: your reactions and attitudes.

When faced with unexpected changes, remind yourself that every challenge is an opportunity to learn and grow. By accepting uncertainty and viewing it as a natural part of life, you can reduce stress and increase your capacity to adapt. Here are some steps to cultivate a positive mindset:

- **Practice Gratitude**: Spend a few minutes each day reflecting on things you are grateful for. This can shift your focus from what is lacking to what is abundant in your life.
- **Surround Yourself with Positivity**: Engage with people who uplift and support you. Read books, listen to podcasts, and watch content that inspires and motivates you.

Build Strong Relationships

No one builds resilience in isolation. Strong social connections and support systems play a crucial role in helping you navigate life's ups and downs. Surround yourself with positive, supportive people who uplift and encourage you.

Building and maintaining strong relationships provides a safety net of emotional support during tough times. Here are some tips:

- **Reach Out**: Don't hesitate to ask for help or talk about your struggles with friends and family. Sharing your experiences can lighten the emotional load.
- **Be a Good Listener**: Building strong relationships also involves being there for others. Practice active listening and empathy.
- **Join Communities**: Engage in communities or groups that share your interests or values. This can provide a sense of belonging and additional support.

Develop Emotional Regulation Skills

Emotional regulation involves managing your emotional responses to stress and adversity. By developing emotional regulation skills, we can approach challenges with a calm and balanced mindset, making it easier to find solutions and move forward. Here are some techniques:

- **Mindfulness and Meditation**: Regular mindfulness practice can help you stay present and reduce the impact of negative emotions. Start with a few minutes of focused breathing or guided meditation each day.
- **Journaling**: Writing about your thoughts and feelings can help you process emotions and gain

clarity. Try setting aside time each day to journal about your experiences.

- **Healthy Outlets**: Engage in activities that help you release stress and improve mood, such as exercise, art, or hobbies.

Enhance Problem-Solving Skills

Effective problem-solving skills are essential for resilience. By clearly defining problems, brainstorming potential solutions, and evaluating their pros and cons, we can make informed decisions and take decisive action. Here are some steps to improve these skills:

- **Identify the Problem**: Clearly define the problem you are facing. This helps in focusing your efforts on finding a solution.
- **Brainstorm Solutions**: Generate a list of potential solutions without judging them initially. Consider all possible options.
- **Evaluate and Act**: Assess the pros and cons of each solution, then choose the best one and take action. Don't be afraid to experiment and learn from the outcome.

Take Care of Your Physical Health

Physical health and emotional well-being are closely linked. Regular exercise, a balanced diet, and adequate sleep are fundamental to maintaining our physical health. Engaging in physical activities we enjoy and setting realistic fitness goals can boost our mood and energy levels. Here are some tips to maintain your physical health:

- **Exercise Regularly**: Aim for at least 30 minutes of physical activity most days of the week. Exercise reduces stress and boosts mood.
- **Healthy Diet**: Eat a balanced diet rich in fruits, vegetables, lean proteins, and whole grains. Avoid excessive caffeine, sugar, and alcohol.
- **Adequate Sleep**: Ensure you get 7-9 hours of sleep each night. Good sleep is essential for emotional regulation and overall health.

Learn from Experience

Every challenge we face is an opportunity to learn and grow. Reflecting on our experiences, identifying lessons learned, and applying these insights to future situations strengthens our resilience. Here's how to make the most of these experiences:

- **Reflect**: After overcoming a challenge, take time to reflect on what you learned. What strategies worked? What could you improve?
- **Apply Lessons**: Use the insights gained from past experiences to inform your approach to future challenges.
- **Share Your Story**: Talking about your experiences can help others and reinforce your own learning. It's a way of turning adversity into something positive.

Maintain a Sense of Humor

Humor can be a powerful tool for resilience. It helps to lighten the mood and provides a different perspective on problems. Here's how to incorporate humor:

- **Find the Funny Side**: Try to see the humor in difficult situations. It can provide relief and a fresh perspective.
- **Laugh Often**: Engage in activities that make you laugh, whether it's watching a comedy, reading a funny book, or spending time with friends who have a good sense of humor.
- **Don't Take Yourself Too Seriously**: Allow yourself to make mistakes and laugh at them. This reduces stress and promotes a positive outlook.

Seek Professional Help When Needed

Sometimes, building resilience requires the support of a professional. Therapists, counselors, and coaches can provide guidance, tools, and strategies to help us navigate challenges more effectively. Recognizing when we need help and seeking it without hesitation is a sign of strength, not weakness. Here's when and how to seek help:

- **Recognize the Signs**: If you're feeling overwhelmed, persistently sad, or anxious, it might be time to seek professional support.

- **Choose the Right Professional**: Look for a therapist, counselor, or coach who specializes in resilience and stress management.
- **Commit to the Process**: Therapy and counseling are processes that take time. Be patient and committed to your personal growth journey.

Building resilience is a journey that requires patience, dedication, and a willingness to grow. It's not about eliminating stress or adversity from your life, but about equipping yourself with the tools to handle these challenges with grace and strength.

By incorporating the strategies into your daily routine, you can foster a resilient mindset that will serve you well in all areas of life. Each step you take towards developing resilience contributes to your overall well-being, enriching your life with a sense of purpose and empowerment.

One of the most encouraging aspects of building resilience is the realization that it is accessible to everyone. Regardless of past experiences or current challenges, resilience can be nurtured through intentional practice. By working on it, you lay the groundwork for a resilient life.

Just as a tree roots itself deeply into the ground to withstand strong winds and storms, we too must establish a strong foundation through positive habits and mindsets. The branches of the tree, flexible yet firm, represent our ability to adapt and grow in response to the changing circumstances of life.

As you work towards building resilience, remember that it is a gradual process. There will be times when you feel strong and capable, and times when you feel overwhelmed. Embrace each moment as part of your growth, and trust that every effort you make is contributing to your overall resilience.

It is about more than just bouncing back from adversity. It is about thriving in the face of challenges, growing stronger with each experience, and living a life filled with purpose and joy.

Resilience is a gift you give to yourself—one that will serve you well throughout your life. By investing in it, you are investing in a future of strength, adaptability, and fulfillment. So take heart, stay committed to your growth, and celebrate the resilient spirit within you.

As you strive to develop resilience, track your progress by answering the following questions.

Weekly Reflection

1. What challenges did I face this week?

2. How did I respond to these challenges?

3. What strategies or exercises did I use to cope?

4. What did I learn from these experiences?

5. What am I grateful for this week?

6. How can I improve my resilience next week?

Monthly Check-in

1. What are the most significant changes you've noticed in yourself?

____

2. How has your understanding of resilience evolved?

____

3. Which strategies were most effective for you, and why?

____

4. How will you continue to practice and build resilience in your daily life?

____

Resources

Books

1. “Resilience: Hard-Won Wisdom for Living a Better Life by Eric Greitens”- A practical guide that combines philosophy, psychology, and military wisdom to offer actionable advice on developing resilience
2. “Facing Adversity, Building Resilience, and Finding Joy” by Sheryl Sandberg and Adam Grant - This book shares personal stories and research-backed strategies for building resilience after experiencing loss and setbacks.

Podcasts

1. "The Resilience Breakthrough Podcast" - Hosted by Christian Moore, this podcast explores various aspects of resilience with guest experts and personal stories.
2. "The Happiness Lab" with Dr. Laurie Santos - While focusing on happiness, this podcast often discusses resilience and strategies for improving mental well-being.

Key Takeaways

- Resilience is the ability to recover from setbacks, adapt to change, and keep moving forward despite adversity, and it can be developed through intentional practice.

- Neuroplasticity, or the brain's ability to adapt and reorganize, plays a significant role in resilience, with practices like mindfulness and gratitude enhancing emotional regulation and stress management.
- Emotional regulation, strong social connections, and a sense of purpose are crucial elements that enable individuals to navigate challenges effectively.
- Resilience is essential not only for overcoming major life challenges but also for managing everyday stressors like work pressure, time constraints, and personal conflicts.
- It helps combat procrastination by fostering confidence and self-discipline while reducing overthinking through mindfulness and constructive action.
- Building resilience requires a holistic approach, addressing physical health with exercise, balanced nutrition, and sleep, while nurturing mental and emotional well-being.
- Practical strategies include cultivating gratitude, focusing on solutions, embracing uncertainty, fostering supportive relationships, and developing effective problem-solving skills.
- Mindfulness practices like meditation and journaling are key tools for regulating emotions, staying present, and managing stress effectively.

- Maintaining a sense of humor helps to lighten stressful situations, shift perspectives, and build resilience.
- Resilient individuals see challenges as opportunities for growth, learn from experiences, and remain adaptable to thrive amidst uncertainty.
- Resilience develops gradually through consistent effort, reflection, and celebrating progress while learning from failures.
- Seeking professional support, such as therapy or counseling, can provide valuable tools and guidance for overcoming significant challenges.
- By fostering resilience, individuals enhance mental health, boost confidence, improve adaptability, strengthen relationships, and achieve greater overall well-being.
- Regular reflection and tracking progress help reinforce positive habits, measure growth, and sustain the practice of building resilience over time.

Chapter 8

Creating A Supportive Environment

Humans are inherently social creatures, deeply influenced by the people around them. As the saying goes, "You are the average of the five people you spend the most time with," a concept popularized by motivational speaker Jim Rohn. This idea underscores the significance of our social circles in molding our behaviors, attitudes, and overall outlook on life.

Research consistently shows that our social environments shape our mental and emotional health. A study by the University of California, San Diego, found that happiness spreads through social networks, suggesting that positive emotions can be contagious among friends and acquaintances.

Conversely, negative influences can also propagate, leading to detrimental effects on mental health and behavior. The Framingham Heart Study, which tracked participants over 20 years, demonstrated that both obesity and smoking habits spread through social ties, underscoring how our connections can influence our health-related behaviors.

The sense of belonging fostered by close relationships is fundamental to our psychological well-being. According to Abraham Maslow's hierarchy of needs, the need for love and belonging is a basic human necessity, critical for self-esteem and self-actualization. When we feel accepted and valued by our social circle, we are more likely to pursue our goals with confidence and determination.

Our closest relationships are pivotal in nurturing our personal and professional growth. When we have friends who inspire us, challenge us, and believe in our potential, we are more likely to push our boundaries and achieve our goals. The encouragement and constructive feedback from a supportive circle can be the catalyst for remarkable growth.

Psychologically, the impact of a supportive environment is profound. Positive reinforcement from loved ones boosts our self-esteem and confidence, making us more resilient to setbacks.

According to psychologist Carl Rogers, unconditional positive regard from others fosters self-worth and self-actualization. This means that when our close circle accepts and supports us unconditionally, we are more likely to thrive and reach our full potential.

Surrounding yourself with support is a powerful strategy for overcoming procrastination and overthinking, two common obstacles that hinder productivity and personal growth.

When we have friends, family, or colleagues who believe in our abilities and offer constructive feedback, we are more likely to feel motivated and less afraid of making mistakes. This encouragement can significantly reduce the anxiety associated with tasks, making it easier to start and complete them.

Supportive relationships also provide accountability, which is crucial for overcoming procrastination. When we share our goals with others and they hold us accountable, we are more likely to follow through.

This sense of responsibility to others can be a powerful motivator. According to a study published in the American Journal of Lifestyle Medicine, accountability partnerships increase the likelihood of achieving goals by up to 95%.

Moreover, a supportive environment helps in managing overthinking by providing perspective. When we are caught in a loop of rumination, talking to someone we trust can help us see the situation more clearly and rationally.

They can offer new insights, challenge our negative thoughts, and help us focus on solutions rather than problems. This external perspective is invaluable in breaking the cycle of overthinking.

Creating a supportive environment also involves cultivating a culture of open communication and mutual support. Encouraging honest conversations about our challenges and fears fosters a sense of community and shared purpose.

When we know that others are facing similar struggles, it normalizes our experiences and reduces the stigma associated with them.

Furthermore, supportive environments often promote healthy habits and routines that counteract procrastination and overthinking. For instance, engaging in group activities like exercise, study sessions, or creative projects can provide structure and reduce the tendency to procrastinate. These activities not only boost productivity but also enhance our mood and overall well-being.

In addition, having a diverse support network can broaden our horizons and stimulate personal growth. Different perspectives and experiences within our circle can challenge our assumptions and encourage innovative thinking. This diversity enriches our lives and fosters a more adaptable and resilient mindset, helping us to tackle procrastination and overthinking with greater agility.

Going beyond the personal and social aspects of a person's life, creating a supportive environment also involves cultivating a positive physical space. Decluttering and organizing our surroundings can enhance focus and reduce distractions. Incorporating elements such as plants, natural light, and comfortable furniture can improve mood and productivity. A study published in the Journal of Environmental Psychology found that individuals working in well-designed environments reported higher levels of well-being and efficiency.

In addition to physical space, incorporating routines and rituals can create a supportive environment. Establishing regular habits, such as dedicated work hours, exercise, and relaxation, can provide structure and reduce the likelihood of procrastination. Routines create a sense of normalcy and predictability, which can alleviate anxiety and promote productivity.

Every interaction we have leaves an impression on our mindset, behavior, and overall well-being. By being conscious of our social interactions, we can curate a positive and supportive environment.

First, it's crucial to identify the types of interactions that uplift and energize us versus those that drain or demotivate us. Positive interactions are characterized by mutual respect, encouragement, and constructive feedback.

Negative interactions, on the other hand, often involve criticism, negativity, and unnecessary stress. Once we recognize these patterns, we can start making intentional choices about who we spend our time with and how we engage with them.

It's not just about choosing the right people, but also about how we interact with them. Setting healthy boundaries, communicating openly, and practicing empathy are key aspects of nurturing positive relationships. Mindful interactions ensure that our social environment is a source of strength and growth rather than a cause of anxiety or distraction.

Setting boundaries in our close relationships is essential for maintaining a healthy balance between personal needs and the expectations of others. Boundaries help protect our emotional and mental well-being, allowing us to focus on our goals and responsibilities without unnecessary interference or stress.

Establishing clear boundaries in our relationships is not just about keeping others out but also about preserving space for ourselves to grow and thrive. Boundaries are a form of self-respect and are essential for maintaining healthy, balanced relationships. They empower us to focus on what truly matters and protect our mental and emotional health. Here's how you can get started:

1. Understand Your Limits: Start by identifying what you need to feel comfortable and respected in your relationships. This could be time alone, specific behaviors you find unacceptable, or certain aspects of your life you wish to keep private.

2. Communicate Clearly: Once you know your limits, communicate them clearly and assertively to your friends, family, or colleagues. Use "I" statements to express your needs without sounding accusatory. For example, "I need some quiet time to focus on my work" instead of "You're always distracting me."

3. Be Consistent: Consistency is key when it comes to boundaries. Enforce your limits consistently to ensure that others understand and respect them. This may involve repeating your boundaries and standing firm even if others push back.

4. Practice Self-Care: Prioritize self-care to reinforce your boundaries. Ensure you are getting enough rest, engaging in activities you enjoy, and taking time for yourself. Self-care strengthens your resolve and helps you maintain your boundaries.

5. Address Boundary Violations: When someone crosses your boundaries, address it calmly but firmly. Explain how their behavior affects you and reiterate your boundary. For instance, "When you call me late at night, it disrupts my sleep. Please try to call earlier in the evening."

6. Seek Support: Sometimes, setting boundaries can be challenging, especially with people who are used to certain dynamics. Seek support from others who respect your boundaries and can offer guidance or reinforcement.

7. Be Patient: Establishing boundaries takes time and patience. People may need time to adjust to the new limits you're setting. Be patient with yourself and others as you navigate this process.

Seeking support from your close circle can be challenging, especially if you're not used to asking for help. However, building a supportive network is crucial for personal and professional growth. People are often hesitant about reaching out to those around us, but it can be incredibly rewarding.

Opening up and asking for help fosters deeper connections and a sense of community. It reminds us that we are not alone in our struggles and that mutual support can be a powerful catalyst for overcoming obstacles and achieving success. Here are steps to break down barriers and open up to seeking support.

1. **Recognize the Need for Support:** The first step is acknowledging that you need help. Understand that seeking support is not a sign of weakness but a proactive step towards growth and well-being.

2. **Identify Trustworthy Individuals:** Think about who in your circle you trust and feel comfortable with. These are the people who are likely to offer genuine support without judgment.

3. **Start Small:** Begin by sharing small concerns or asking for minor favors. This helps build trust and makes it easier to ask for more significant support later on.

4. **Be Honest and Vulnerable:** Open up about your struggles and be honest about what you need. Vulnerability fosters deeper connections and allows others to understand and support you better.

5. **Use Clear Communication:** Clearly articulate what kind of support you're looking for. Whether it's advice, a listening ear, or practical help, being specific

makes it easier for others to provide the right kind of support.

6. Show Appreciation: Acknowledge and appreciate the support you receive. Gratitude strengthens relationships and encourages ongoing support.

7. Offer Support in Return: Building a supportive network is reciprocal. Offer your support to others when they need it, creating a culture of mutual aid.

8. Join Support Groups or Communities: Sometimes, support can come from outside your immediate circle. Consider joining groups or communities where you can connect with people who share similar experiences and challenges.

Creating a conducive space for productivity involves a combination of physical organization, mental preparedness, and personal comfort. A well-designed workspace can significantly enhance focus, efficiency, and overall performance. Designing a space for productivity is about more than just physical organization; it's about crafting an environment that motivates and energizes you.

Here are tips and pointers to help you set up an environment that maximizes your productivity:

1. Designate a Workspace: Establishing a specific area solely for work or study is the first step in creating a productive environment. This space should be separate from areas associated with leisure or relaxation, such as your bedroom or living room. A designated workspace signals to your brain that it's time to focus and be productive.

2. Keep it Organized: An organized workspace is crucial for maintaining focus and reducing stress. Clutter can be distracting and overwhelming, leading to decreased productivity. Ensure that your desk is clean and only contains essential items. Use storage solutions like drawers, shelves, and organizers to keep supplies and documents neatly arranged.

Regularly declutter your space to maintain a tidy environment. A study by Princeton University Neuroscience Institute found that physical clutter in your surroundings competes for your attention, resulting in decreased performance and increased stress.

3. Ensure Comfort: Comfort is a key factor in sustaining long periods of focus. Invest in ergonomic furniture that supports good posture and reduces physical strain. A comfortable chair with proper lumbar support and a desk at the right height can prevent back and neck pain.

Additionally, ensure that your workspace has adequate lighting to reduce eye strain and fatigue. Natural light is ideal, but if that's not possible, use bright, adjustable desk lamps.

4. Minimize Distractions: Identify and eliminate potential distractions to maintain a focused work environment. This might involve setting boundaries with family members or roommates, such as establishing quiet hours or using a do-not-disturb sign.

Turn off notifications on your phone or computer and use apps that block access to distracting websites during work hours. Noise-canceling headphones can also help minimize auditory distractions.

5. Use a Schedule: Creating a structured schedule helps manage your time effectively. Allocate specific time blocks for different tasks and adhere to this schedule as closely as possible. Techniques like time blocking or the Pomodoro Technique can boost productivity and prevent burnout.

6. Take Breaks: Regular breaks are essential for maintaining high levels of productivity and preventing mental fatigue. Short, frequent breaks help refresh your mind and improve focus. Use break time to stretch, walk around, or engage in a brief relaxing activity.

Taking breaks can actually increase your overall productivity by preventing burnout and maintaining a high level of concentration.

7. Personalize Your Space: Adding personal touches to your workspace can make it more inviting and inspiring. Decorate your desk with items that motivate you, such as plants, artwork, or inspirational quotes. A personalized space can boost your mood, creativity, and overall satisfaction with your work environment.

8. Manage Noise Levels: Noise levels can significantly impact your ability to concentrate. Identify your preferred noise environment—some people work best in complete silence, while others might prefer background noise or music. Use noise-canceling headphones to block out disruptive sounds or play instrumental music or white noise to create a more focused atmosphere.

9. Maintain a Healthy Routine: Your physical well-being directly affects your productivity. Incorporate healthy habits into your daily routine, such as regular exercise, adequate sleep, and proper nutrition.

Staying hydrated and taking care of your body ensures that you have the energy and focus needed to be productive. Simple practices like starting your day with a healthy breakfast and taking short exercise breaks can make a significant difference.

10. Technology and Tools: Leverage technology and tools to enhance your productivity. Use digital calendars, task management apps, and note-taking tools to organize your work and stay on top of deadlines.

Tools like Notion can also facilitate collaboration and streamline workflows. However, be mindful not to overrely on technology, as it can become a distraction if not used effectively.

11. Flexibility and Adaptability: Be open to adjusting your workspace and routines as needed. Productivity is not a one-size-fits-all concept, and what works best for you may change over time. Regularly assess your productivity levels and make adjustments to your environment and habits to continually optimize your workspace.

As the saying goes, "Birds of a feather flock together." By being mindful of who we spend our time with and how we interact, we can create a network that fuels our ambitions and nurtures our well-being.

Embrace the power of a supportive network, the clarity of well-defined boundaries, and the comfort of a productive workspace. Together, these elements form the bedrock of a fulfilling, balanced, and successful life. So, take these steps with confidence and watch as your environment transforms, paving the way for your personal and professional growth.

Resources

Books

- "Deep Work" by Cal Newport - While the core focus is on deep work, it extensively discusses the importance of creating distraction-free environments for optimal productivity.
- "Mindset: The New Psychology of Success by Carol Dweck" - This book discusses the importance of a growth mindset which can significantly influence how you interact with and perceive your environment, affecting productivity.

Key Takeaways

- Surrounding yourself with positive and supportive individuals profoundly impacts mental health, resilience, and personal growth.
- A sense of belonging and encouragement from close relationships fosters confidence, reduces procrastination, and promotes accountability.
- Sharing concerns with trusted people offers fresh perspectives, helping to break overthinking cycles and focus on solutions.
- Curating a supportive network involves open communication, mutual respect, and setting healthy boundaries to maintain emotional well-being.

- A well-designed, distraction-free workspace tailored to comfort and functionality enhances focus, efficiency, and productivity.
- Establishing routines and leveraging tools like time management apps provide structure and reduce procrastination.
- Flexibility in routines and workspace design ensures adaptability and long-term productivity.
- A supportive environment in relationships, habits, and physical spaces forms the foundation for a balanced and fulfilling life.

Chapter 9

Finding Purpose and Motivation

At some point in life, most of us have felt lost, unsure of what we truly want. It's a universal experience, one that often leaves us feeling stuck or adrift. Whether we're just starting out in our careers, transitioning to a new phase of life, or simply re-evaluating our current path, the question of purpose can seem elusive.

This feeling isn't a sign of failure; rather, it's a natural part of the human journey. The uncertainty we experience can be a powerful motivator for growth and self-discovery. Understanding that this state of confusion is common can be reassuring, reminding us that we're not alone in our quest for meaning.

Purpose is a fundamental aspect of human existence. It refers to a sense of direction and meaning in life, guiding our actions, decisions, and long-term goals.

Renowned psychiatrist Viktor Frankl, in his book *Man's Search for Meaning*, stated, "Life is never made unbearable by circumstances, but only by lack of meaning and purpose."

Research supports the significance of purpose in enhancing overall well-being. According to a study published in the journal *Psychological Science*, individuals with a strong sense of purpose tend to live longer, healthier lives. Purpose is more than just a goal; it is a compass that provides direction, sustains motivation, and fosters resilience against life's challenges.

Ikigai, a Japanese concept, translates to "a reason for being" and represents the intersection of what you love, what you are good at, what the world needs, and what you can be paid for. It is a holistic approach to finding purpose and fulfillment in life. By identifying your ikigai, you can align your passions, skills, values, and the needs of the world, creating a balanced and meaningful life.

This alignment not only enhances personal satisfaction and happiness but also fosters a sense of contribution and significance. Embracing ikigai involves continuous self-reflection and adjustment, ensuring that your daily activities and long-term goals resonate with your deepest motivations and aspirations.

Having a clear purpose transforms life in profound ways. It acts as an anchor, providing stability and a sense of direction even in turbulent times. When one is driven by purpose, decisions become easier to make, and actions more deliberate.

Purpose helps individuals prioritize their efforts, focusing on what truly matters and aligning their daily activities with their long-term aspirations.

Moreover, purpose fuels motivation. It ignites a passion that propels individuals forward, even when faced with obstacles. The energy derived from knowing one's purpose can make the difference between persisting through difficulties and giving up. This intrinsic motivation is often more powerful and enduring than external rewards or incentives.

Purpose also enhances resilience. People with a strong sense of purpose are better equipped to handle stress and setbacks. They view challenges as opportunities for growth rather than insurmountable barriers. This positive outlook not only improves mental health but also fosters a proactive approach to problem-solving and personal development.

Furthermore, purpose fosters a sense of fulfillment and satisfaction. Engaging in meaningful activities and pursuing goals that resonate with one's values leads to a deeper sense of contentment. This fulfillment is not merely about achieving success but about the journey itself—finding joy and significance in each step taken toward one's aspirations.

Some buzzwords that are often thrown around with purpose are “values”, “passion” and “long-term objectives". Let's take a close look at what they really mean.

Values are the fundamental beliefs and principles that guide our behavior and decision-making. They represent what is most important to us in life and serve as the foundation for our actions and attitudes.

Identifying and understanding your core values is crucial for aligning your life with what truly matters to you. When you live according to your values, you experience greater integrity, satisfaction, and coherence in your life. Reflecting on your values helps you make decisions that are consistent with your beliefs, leading to a more authentic and fulfilling life.

Passion refers to the intense enthusiasm and excitement we feel for certain activities, topics, or pursuits. It is what drives us to engage deeply and persistently with our interests, often leading to a state of flow where we lose track of time and feel fully immersed.

Discovering and nurturing your passions is vital for achieving a sense of purpose and motivation. When you pursue what you are passionate about, you are more likely to experience joy, fulfillment, and a strong sense of personal identity. Passion fuels your motivation and resilience, enabling you to overcome obstacles and persist in the face of challenges.

Long-term goals are the aspirations and objectives that we strive to achieve over an extended period. They provide direction and structure to our lives, helping us focus our efforts on what is most important. Setting and pursuing long-term goals requires careful planning and sustained effort, but the rewards are substantial.

These goals often align with our values and passions, making them deeply meaningful and motivating. By defining your long-term goals, you create a roadmap for your future, guiding your actions and decisions toward a fulfilling and purposeful life.

Now that we have a basic understanding, let's dive into some questions that could be cues to identifying your purpose. Some of the reflective questions are designed to provoke thought and elicit deep responses.

They help you explore your experiences, feelings, and aspirations, providing insight into your true self. Answering these questions can reveal patterns and themes that highlight your values and passions.

What activities or experiences make you feel most alive and engaged?

This question helps you identify what excites and energizes you. Recognizing these activities can guide you toward pursuits that bring joy and fulfillment.

What values are most important to you in life (e.g., honesty, creativity, compassion)?

Identifying your core values is crucial because they serve as a foundation for your decisions and actions. Aligning your life with these values leads to greater satisfaction and integrity.

Think about moments when you felt truly fulfilled. What were you doing?

Reflecting on past experiences of fulfillment can reveal your passions and strengths. Understanding these moments can help you replicate similar experiences in the future.

If you had no constraints (financial, time, etc.), what would you spend your time doing?

This question removes practical barriers and allows you to dream freely. It helps you uncover your deepest desires and aspirations, providing a clearer vision of what you truly want in life.

Engaging in exercises can further clarify your values, passions, and long-term goals. These activities offer a structured approach to self-discovery, making the abstract concept of purpose more tangible.

Values Clarification Exercise

- **Steps**: List your core values and rank them in order of importance. Reflect on how these values influence your decisions and actions.
- **How this will help**: This exercise helps you prioritize what matters most to you. By understanding your values, you can make more aligned and meaningful choices in your life.

Passion Exploration Exercise

- **Steps**: Write down all the activities and topics that interest you. Highlight those that you are most passionate about and consider how you can incorporate them into your daily life.
- **How this will help**: Identifying your passions enables you to pursue activities that bring joy and fulfillment. This exercise helps integrate your interests into your routine, enhancing your overall happiness.

Vision Board

- **Steps**: Create a visual representation of your goals and aspirations using images, quotes, and symbols. This can help clarify your vision and keep you motivated.
- **How this will help**: A vision board serves as a constant reminder of your goals and dreams. It keeps you focused and inspired, making it easier to stay on track and motivated.

In our fast-paced world, the struggle with procrastination and the quest for sustained motivation are common challenges. Many people find themselves caught in a cycle of delayed actions and unfulfilled aspirations, leading to stress and dissatisfaction. A powerful approach to overcoming these hurdles is aligning one's actions with their core values. When actions are congruent with values, they become more meaningful and engaging, fostering a natural drive to act and reducing the tendency to procrastinate.

Motivation is the driving force that propels us to take action and pursue our goals. It is often categorized into two types: intrinsic and extrinsic. Intrinsic motivation arises from within, driven by personal satisfaction and fulfillment, while extrinsic motivation is driven by external rewards or pressures.

Motivation is often driven by the significance we attach to our actions. When we engage in activities aligned with our values, we inherently find them more fulfilling and rewarding. This alignment creates intrinsic motivation, where the activity itself is enjoyable and worthwhile, rather than relying on external rewards or pressures. Intrinsic motivation is more sustainable and resilient, helping individuals maintain enthusiasm and commitment over the long term.

For example, consider a person whose core value is creativity. If their work or hobbies involve creative expression, they are likely to feel more motivated and energized. This intrinsic drive makes it easier to start and continue tasks, reducing the inclination to procrastinate. Conversely, when actions are misaligned with values, they feel like chores, draining energy and leading to avoidance behaviors.

Research supports this connection. A study published in the *Journal of Counseling Psychology* found that individuals who pursued goals aligned with their intrinsic values reported higher levels of motivation and well-being. This alignment fosters a deeper engagement with the activity, making it more rewarding and less likely to be deferred.

Purpose is closely tied to values and plays a crucial role in combating procrastination. When we have a clear sense of purpose, our actions are directed toward meaningful goals that resonate with our values. This sense of direction provides clarity and focus, making it easier to prioritize tasks and avoid distractions.

Procrastination often stems from a lack of clarity or connection to our goals. When tasks feel arbitrary or disconnected from our values, it is harder to find the motivation to start. By aligning tasks with a broader purpose, we create a compelling reason to act, which helps overcome inertia and procrastination.

While aligning actions with values is a powerful strategy for enhancing motivation and reducing procrastination, it is not without challenges. Understanding and addressing these challenges can help ensure that you stay true to your values and continue to make meaningful progress toward your goals. Here are some common obstacles and strategies for overcoming them:

Value Conflicts

Sometimes, different values may come into conflict with each other, making it difficult to decide which action to prioritize. For instance, you might value both family and career success, but find that dedicating time to one comes at the expense of the other.

Strategies to Overcome Value Conflicts:

1. **Prioritize and Balance:** Reflect on the relative importance of each value in the context of your current situation. Prioritize actions that align with your most critical values at this moment while finding ways to incorporate other values when possible. For example, if a career project demands extra time, look for ways to include family time in less demanding periods.

2. **Seek Integration:** Find ways to integrate conflicting values. For instance, if you value both health and social connection, consider engaging in physical activities with friends or family, such as hiking or playing sports together.

3. **Set Boundaries:** Establish clear boundaries to protect your most important values. Communicate your limits to others and be firm about allocating time and resources in a way that honors your priorities.

External Pressures

Societal expectations, peer pressure, and external demands can distract you from your values and lead you to make choices that do not align with your true self.

Strategies to Overcome External Pressures:

1. **Strengthen Self-awareness:** Regularly reflect on your values and reaffirm your commitment to them. Mindfulness and journaling can help you stay connected to your inner beliefs and resist external influences.
2. **Develop Assertiveness:** Learn to assertively communicate your values and boundaries to others. Practice saying "no" to requests or opportunities that do not align with your core values, and explain your reasoning when necessary.
3. **Surround Yourself with Support:** Build a network of supportive individuals who respect and share your values. Seek out mentors, friends, or communities that encourage you to stay true to yourself and provide reinforcement when you face external pressures.

Internal Doubts

Self-doubt and fear of failure can undermine efforts to live according to your values, leading to procrastination and avoidance.

Strategies to Overcome Internal Doubts:

1. **Cultivate a Growth Mindset:** Embrace a growth mindset, which views challenges and failures as opportunities for learning and development. Remind yourself that setbacks are

part of the journey and do not define your worth or capabilities.

2. **Practice Self-compassion:** Be kind and patient with yourself when you encounter difficulties. Acknowledge your efforts and progress, even if they are small, and avoid harsh self-criticism.
3. **Seek Feedback and Encouragement:** Share your goals and challenges with trusted friends, family, or mentors. Their positive feedback and encouragement can boost your confidence and help you stay focused on your values.

Time Management

Balancing multiple responsibilities and demands can make it challenging to prioritize actions that align with your values.

Strategies to Overcome Time Management Challenges:

1. **Effective Prioritization:** Use time management techniques such as the Eisenhower Matrix to categorize tasks based on their urgency and importance. Prioritize tasks that are both important and aligned with your values.
2. **Create a Value-driven Schedule:** Allocate specific times in your schedule for activities that

reflect your values. For example, if health is a core value, schedule regular exercise sessions and treat them as non-negotiable appointments.

3. **Eliminate Time-wasters:** Identify activities that consume time without contributing to your values or goals, such as excessive social media use or unproductive meetings. Minimize or eliminate these time-wasters to free up time for more meaningful actions.

Maintaining Consistency

Staying consistent in aligning actions with values can be difficult, especially when faced with changing circumstances or temptations.

Strategies to Maintain Consistency:

1. **Regular Reflection and Adjustment:** Periodically review your values and goals to ensure they remain relevant and aligned with your current situation. Adjust your action plans as needed to stay on track.
2. **Use Visual Reminders:** Keep reminders of your values and goals in visible places, such as your workspace or home. Vision boards, quotes, or symbols can serve as constant motivators and keep you focused on your purpose.
3. **Develop Habits and Routines:** Establish daily or weekly routines that incorporate actions aligned with your values. Consistent habits

reduce the mental effort required to make value-driven choices and help sustain long-term commitment.

4. **Reward Yourself:** Celebrate your achievements and progress, no matter how small. Positive reinforcement helps maintain motivation.

Aligning your actions with your core values is a transformative journey that paves the way for a more fulfilling and motivated life. It's about understanding what truly matters to you and making conscious choices that reflect those priorities.

By doing so, you can unlock a profound sense of purpose and intrinsic motivation, which naturally diminishes the tendency to procrastinate. While the path may present challenges, such as value conflicts, external pressures, and internal doubts, these obstacles are surmountable with self-awareness, strategic planning, and supportive networks.

The process of discovering and following your values, setting value-based goals, and integrating them into your actions might seem challenging at first.

However, the rewards are immense. You will find that your decisions become easier, your path clearer, and your sense of fulfillment deeper. When your actions reflect your true self, you are more likely to experience joy and satisfaction, even in the face of obstacles.

Remember, this journey is personal and unique to you. It's okay to take small steps and make gradual changes. Celebrate each bit of progress and be kind to yourself when things don't go perfectly. Reflect regularly on your values and goals, adjust your plans as needed, and stay connected to what truly matters to you.

Most importantly, trust in your ability to create a life that is meaningful and aligned with your values. With patience, persistence, and self-awareness, you can overcome challenges, stay motivated, and live a purpose-driven life that brings you joy and fulfillment. So, start today—reflect on your values, set your goals, and take the first step towards a more motivated and purposeful life. You've got this!

Resources

Books

1. "Man's Search for Meaning" by Viktor E. Frankl - A profound exploration of finding meaning and purpose in life, even in the most challenging circumstances.
2. "The Power of Full Engagement" by Jim Loehr and Tony Schwartz - This book focuses on managing energy rather than time and aligning actions with personal values to achieve high performance and personal renewal.
3. "Ikigai: The Japanese Secret to a Long and Happy Life" by Héctor García and Francesc Miralles - This book explores the concept of ikigai and how it can help you find purpose, happiness, and a long life through the lessons from the Japanese culture, particularly the residents of Okinawa.

Podcasts

1. "The Tim Ferriss Show" - Hosted by Tim Ferriss, this podcast features interviews with successful people from various fields, discussing their routines, values, and how they find motivation and purpose.
2. "On Purpose with Jay Shetty" - Jay Shetty shares insights and interviews with thought leaders to

help listeners find purpose and live a more meaningful life.

3. "The Good Life Project" - Hosted by Jonathan Fields, this podcast explores what it means to live a good life, with conversations that delve into finding purpose, meaning, and motivation.

Key Takeaways

- Purpose provides direction, intrinsic motivation, and resilience, leading to a fulfilling life.
- Ikigai aligns passions, skills, values, and societal needs to create meaning.
- Reflecting on core values, moments of fulfillment, and what excites you helps uncover purpose.
- Aligning actions with values reduces procrastination and fosters deeper motivation.
- Overcoming challenges like value conflicts and self-doubt requires self-awareness, prioritization, and supportive networks.
- Consistency in purpose-driven actions can be maintained through habits, reflection, and celebrating progress.

Chapter 10

Overcoming Overwhelm

Feeling overwhelmed is an all-too-familiar experience for many people in today's world. It's a sensation that can creep in slowly or hit like a tidal wave, leaving us feeling paralyzed and unsure of where to begin. Albert Einstein once said, "Out of clutter, find simplicity." This quote resonates deeply today as many of us struggle to find that simplicity amidst the chaos.

Feeling overwhelmed is a natural response to having too much on our plates. It's a common experience that doesn't discriminate; it affects students, professionals, parents, and retirees alike. Research from the Anxiety and Depression Association of America (ADAA) indicates that approximately 40 million adults in the United States experience an anxiety disorder, often exacerbated by overwhelming responsibilities.

Procrastination and overthinking are two significant contributors to the feeling of overwhelm. Procrastination, often seen as a simple lack of willpower or laziness, is much more complex. It's a coping mechanism that people use to deal with the anxiety and stress of starting or completing a task.

Timothy Pychyl, a procrastination researcher, notes that "procrastination is an emotional regulation problem, not a time management problem."

Overthinking, on the other hand, involves dwelling on problems or tasks to the point where it hinders our ability to take action. This habit can lead to analysis paralysis, where the fear of making the wrong decision prevents us from making any decision at all.

According to Susan Nolen-Hoeksema, a psychologist who extensively studied the impact of overthinking, "Ruminators are less likely to take action and solve their problems."

Both procrastination and overthinking are fueled by a fear of failure, a lack of confidence, and a desire for perfectionism. When we believe that we must perform perfectly or that the outcome must be flawless, the pressure becomes overwhelming, leading us to avoid tasks altogether or to obsess over them without making progress.

These patterns are self-reinforcing. The more we procrastinate or overthink, the more our tasks pile up, increasing our sense of overwhelm and making it even harder to start. Breaking this cycle requires a shift in mindset and the development of new habits that promote action and reduce stress.

Managing overwhelm isn't about eradicating stress entirely but rather about developing effective strategies to cope with and reduce it. Whether you're tackling a mountain of tasks at work, balancing personal responsibilities, or simply trying to navigate daily life, there are actionable steps you can take to regain control and find peace. Let's delve into a variety of strategies, exercises, and tips designed to help you break tasks down into smaller, more manageable steps and reduce the overall sense of being overwhelmed.

These methods are simple, easy to implement, and can make a significant difference in how you approach and handle your to-do list.

1. Break Tasks into Smaller Steps

One of the most effective ways to manage overwhelm is to break down tasks into smaller, more manageable steps. Instead of viewing a project as a single, daunting entity, divide it into individual components. For instance, writing a report can be broken down into researching the topic, creating an outline, drafting sections, and revising the final document. By focusing on one small step at a time, the task becomes less intimidating and more achievable.

2. Prioritize and Create a To-Do List

Creating a prioritized to-do list can help clarify what needs to be done and in what order. Start by listing all the tasks you need to accomplish, then rank them based on their urgency and importance.

Use tools like the Eisenhower Matrix to categorize tasks into four quadrants: urgent and important, important but not urgent, urgent but not important, and neither urgent nor important. This method helps you focus on what truly matters and avoid getting bogged down by less critical tasks.

3. Delegate and Ask for Help

Recognize that you don't have to do everything on your own. Delegating tasks and asking for help can alleviate some of the burdens and make your workload more manageable.

Whether it's at work or at home, identify tasks that can be shared or outsourced and communicate your needs to others. Collaborating with colleagues, friends, or family members can provide support and reduce feelings of overwhelm.

4. Establish a Routine

Having a consistent routine can create a sense of structure and predictability, which can be comforting when you're feeling overwhelmed. Establish regular times for work, breaks, meals, and relaxation. A well-structured day can help you manage your time more effectively and reduce the stress of having too many tasks vying for your attention.

In the chaos of this world, self-care and stress management are more critical than ever. They are not just buzzwords; they are essential practices that can significantly improve your quality of life. Balancing the demands of work, family, and personal time can be challenging, but by prioritizing self-care and effectively managing stress, you can maintain both mental and physical well-being.

Taking care of yourself is not just a luxury—it's a necessity. In the midst of our busy lives, it's easy to neglect our own needs in favor of meeting deadlines, taking care of others, or simply keeping up with the demands of daily life.

However, prioritizing self-care is essential for maintaining both your physical health and your mental well-being. It's about recognizing your worth and taking deliberate steps to nurture yourself. As the famous saying goes, "You can't pour from an empty cup." Taking time for self-care allows you to recharge and be more effective in all areas of your life.

A study published in *BMC Health Services Research* found that healthcare professionals who practiced regular self-care experienced lower levels of stress and burnout. This underscores that self-care is not just about feeling good in the moment; it has long-term benefits for overall health and well-being.

Stress management is equally important. Chronic stress can have detrimental effects on your health, including increasing the risk of conditions like heart disease, diabetes, and depression. Effective stress management helps to mitigate these risks and promotes a healthier, more balanced life.

Techniques such as mindfulness, exercise, and adequate rest can significantly reduce stress levels. According to a study by the American Psychological Association, individuals who engage in regular physical activity report lower levels of stress and better overall mental health.

Integrating self-care and stress management into your daily routine can lead to a more balanced and fulfilling life.

Here are some key aspects to consider:

1. **Physical Health**: Regular exercise, a balanced diet, and sufficient sleep are foundational to good health. Exercise, in particular, is a powerful stress reliever. The Mayo Clinic highlights that physical activity increases the production of endorphins, which are natural mood lifters.

2. **Mental Health**: Practices such as mindfulness meditation, journaling, and spending time in nature can improve mental well-being. A study from Harvard Medical School found that mindfulness meditation can decrease stress and

anxiety, highlighting its effectiveness as a stress management tool.

3. **Emotional Health**: Building strong relationships and seeking social support are vital. Talking to friends, family, or a therapist can provide relief and perspective when dealing with stress.
4. **Professional Boundaries**: Learning to set boundaries at work is crucial for preventing burnout. This includes knowing when to say no and taking breaks when needed.
5. **Leisure and Hobbies**: Engaging in activities you enjoy can provide a necessary break from daily stressors. Whether it's reading, gardening, or painting, hobbies can be a great way to relax and recharge.

Incorporating these elements into your life doesn't require drastic changes. Small, consistent steps can lead to significant improvements in how you manage stress and care for yourself.

Now that we understand the importance of self-care and stress management, let's explore some easy exercises you can incorporate into your daily routine.

Deep Breathing Exercises - Deep breathing is a simple yet powerful tool for stress relief. It activates the body's relaxation response, helping to reduce stress and anxiety. Try the following exercise:

- **4-7-8 Breathing**: Inhale through your nose for 4 seconds, hold your breath for 7 seconds, and exhale through your mouth for 8 seconds. Repeat this cycle 3-4 times.

Social Connection - Spending time with loved ones can be a great stress reliever. Make an effort to connect with friends and family regularly:

- Schedule regular phone calls or video chats with loved ones.
- Plan social activities that you enjoy, such as a coffee date or a game night.
- Join clubs or groups that share your interests to meet new people.

Create a Relaxing Evening Routine - End your day on a peaceful note by creating a calming evening routine. This could include activities such as:

- **Reading a book**: Choose a genre that you find enjoyable and immerse yourself in a good story.
- **Taking a warm bath**: Add soothing bath salts or essential oils to help you unwind.
- **Practicing gentle yoga or stretching**: Release tension from your body and quiet your mind.
- **Listening to calming music or nature sounds**: Create a tranquil atmosphere to promote relaxation.

Schedule Regular Exercise - Physical activity is not only beneficial for your body but also for your mental health. Find activities that you enjoy and make them a regular part of your routine:

- **Walking or jogging**: Take a brisk walk in nature or jog around your neighborhood.
- **Dancing**: Put on your favorite music and dance like nobody's watching.
- **Yoga or Pilates**: Improve flexibility and strength while promoting relaxation.
- **Home workouts**: Follow online workout videos or create your own routine using bodyweight exercises.

Connect with Nature - Spending time outdoors can have a rejuvenating effect on your mind and body. Make time to connect with nature:

- **Go for a hike or nature walk**: Explore nearby trails or parks and appreciate the beauty of the natural world.
- **Gardening**: Plant flowers or vegetables, and enjoy the therapeutic benefits of working with soil.
- **Picnic in the park**: Pack a lunch and relax in a peaceful outdoor setting.

Nourish Your Body with Healthy Food - Eating a balanced diet provides essential nutrients for your physical and mental well-being. Focus on incorporating nutritious foods into your meals:

- **Prepare homemade meals**: Cook simple, healthy recipes using fresh ingredients.
- **Stay hydrated**: Drink plenty of water throughout the day to maintain optimal hydration.
- **Enjoy mindful eating**: Slow down and savor each bite, paying attention to flavors and textures.

Create a Self-Care Jar - Gather a collection of small, folded pieces of paper and write different self-care activities on each one. Whenever you need a moment of self-care, randomly pick a paper from the jar and do the activity written on it. Examples include:

- **30-minute tech detox**: Disconnect from screens and enjoy uninterrupted time for relaxation.
- **Self-massage with essential oils**: Use soothing oils like lavender or peppermint to massage your hands or feet.
- **Dance party for one**: Put on your favorite upbeat music and dance freely to lift your spirits.

Practice Digital Detox - Give yourself a break from digital devices and the constant stream of information:

- **Set designated screen-free times**: Establish periods during the day when you disconnect from devices.
- **Engage in analog activities**: Read a physical book, write in a journal with pen and paper, or engage in hobbies that don't involve screens.
- **Go tech-free on weekends**: Dedicate weekends to unplugging from technology and focusing on activities that nourish your soul.

Explore Sound Therapy - Sound therapy involves using sound frequencies to promote relaxation and healing. Try incorporating sound therapy into your self-care routine:

- **Listen to calming music**: Explore genres like classical, ambient, or nature sounds that help you relax.
- **Use singing bowls or tuning forks**: Experiment with these instruments to experience their therapeutic vibrations.
- **Attend sound bath sessions**: Look for local events or online sessions where you can immerse yourself in soothing sounds.

Volunteer or Perform Random Acts of Kindness - Giving back to others can be a fulfilling way to practice self-care:

- **Volunteer your time**: Find opportunities to support causes or organizations that are meaningful to you.
- **Perform random acts of kindness**: Pay for someone's coffee, leave a kind note for a neighbor, or offer assistance to someone in need.
- **Join community service projects**: Participate in community clean-ups, food drives, or other initiatives that contribute to the well-being of others

Engage in Art Therapy - Express yourself creatively through art therapy to reduce stress and enhance self-awareness:

- **Painting or drawing**: Use art materials to create visual representations of your emotions or experiences.
- **Coloring books for adults**: Explore intricate designs and patterns in coloring books designed for stress relief.
- **Collage-making**: Create collages using images and words that reflect your thoughts, feelings, and aspirations.

Finding time for self-care in a busy schedule can be tough. We often feel pulled in so many directions that it seems impossible to squeeze in any "me time." But making self-care a priority means carving out even small moments just for you.

It's about understanding that taking care of your own needs isn't selfish—it's essential. When we look after ourselves, we're more resilient and effective in all our roles, benefiting not just ourselves but also those around us.

There is no one-size-fits-all approach to self-care. What works wonders for one person might not resonate with another. That's why it's important to experiment and find out what truly makes you happy and replenishes your energy.

Maybe it's a quiet morning walk, a few minutes of meditation, or indulging in a favorite hobby. Perhaps it's connecting with loved ones, reading a good book, or simply taking a break from digital screens. The key is to listen to your own needs and preferences, discovering practices that bring you joy and peace.

As you explore different self-care practices, remember that you deserve this time and attention. You deserve to feel joy and contentment. Self-care is not an indulgence; it's a necessary foundation for a fulfilling and balanced life. By investing in yourself, you're building a reservoir of strength and positivity that enhances every aspect of your existence.

So, give yourself permission to put yourself first. Make self-care a non-negotiable part of your routine. Be gentle with yourself during the process. It's about continually nurturing your well-being and finding what works best for you at any given time. Ultimately, taking care of yourself is an act of self-love and respect.

It's a declaration that your well-being matters. Embrace this journey with an open heart, knowing that you are worthy of the time, effort, and joy that self-care brings. Prioritize yourself, experiment with different practices, and cherish the moments of peace and happiness they bring. You deserve it.

Self-Care Template

If you're feeling lost about where to start with self-care, don't worry. Everyone needs a little guidance now and then. To help you begin, here's a simple and comprehensive template you can refer to.

This plan is designed to make self-care straightforward and achievable, setting you on a path to better well-being.

Daily Self-Care Plan

Morning Routine:

1. **Hydrate:** Drink a glass of water upon waking up.
2. **Stretch:** Spend 5 minutes stretching or doing light yoga.
3. **Gratitude:** Think of or write down one thing you're grateful for.
4. **Affirmation:** Recite a positive affirmation to start your day.

Throughout the Day:

1. **Breaks:** Take short breaks every hour to rest your eyes and mind.
2. **Breathing:** Practice deep breathing exercises for 2 minutes when feeling stressed.
3. **Nutrition:** Eat balanced meals and keep healthy snacks on hand.
4. **Movement:** Incorporate small movements, like a quick walk or desk exercises.

Evening Routine:

1. **Disconnect:** Turn off screens at least an hour before bed.
2. **Reflection:** Journal about your day or write down three positive things.
3. **Relaxation:** Spend 10 minutes doing a calming activity like reading or listening to music.
4. **Sleep Hygiene:** Establish a consistent bedtime routine.

Weekly Self-Care Plan

Physical Activity:

1. **Exercise:** Aim for at least 30 minutes of physical activity three times a week (e.g., walking, yoga, gym).

2. **Outdoor Time:** Spend time outdoors at least once a week.

Social Connections:

1. **Quality Time:** Schedule time with friends or family (e.g., coffee date, phone call).
2. **Community:** Engage in a community activity or group.

Personal Growth:

1. **Learning:** Dedicate time to learn something new (e.g., reading, online course).
2. **Hobbies:** Spend time on a hobby or creative activity.

Self-Reflection:

1. **Weekly Check-In:** Reflect on your week and adjust your self-care plan as needed.

Monthly Self-Care Plan

Health and Wellness:

1. **Appointments:** Schedule any necessary medical or dental check-ups.
2. **Self-Assessment:** Review your physical and mental health.

Personal Time:

1. **Day for Yourself:** Plan a day dedicated to self-care activities (e.g., spa day, hiking, stay-at-home relaxation).
2. **New Experience:** Try something new or go on a small adventure.

Financial Wellness:

1. **Budget Review:** Review and adjust your budget.
2. **Financial Goals:** Set or review short-term and long-term financial goals.

Environment:

1. **Declutter:** Spend time organizing and decluttering your space.
2. **Home Improvement:** Make a small improvement to your living environment.

Resources

Books

1. "The Self-Care Solution" by Jennifer Ashton, M.D. - Offers monthly self-care challenges to improve your health and well-being.
2. “How to Do Nothing: Resisting the Attention Economy" by Jenny Odell - Advocates for the importance of taking time to disconnect and focus on personal well-being.
3. “The Happiness Project" by Gretchen Rubin - Chronicles the author’s year-long journey to improve her happiness through various self-care strategies.

Key Takeaways

- Feeling overwhelmed often stems from procrastination, overthinking, and perfectionism, which create a cycle of stress and inaction.
- Breaking tasks into smaller, manageable steps and prioritizing them reduces the sense of overwhelm.
- Delegating tasks and asking for help can lighten the load and improve productivity.
- Establishing routines and setting boundaries provides structure and predictability, helping to manage responsibilities effectively.

- Self-care is essential for mental and physical well-being; practices like mindfulness, exercise, and sleep support resilience against stress.
- Managing overwhelm includes addressing emotional and physical health through consistent routines and regular reflection on progress.
- Regular self-care activities, such as deep breathing, spending time in nature, and connecting with loved ones, are crucial for reducing stress and maintaining balance.
- Finding time for self-care requires intentional prioritization and understanding that it is foundational to overall well-being.

About the Author

Sushant Rajput is an award-winning author of '*I Wish Someone Told Me This Before My First Job*.' His debut book has garnered several literary accolades, including being recognized as an 'Amazon Bestseller.'

An accomplished management professional with over two decades of experience in the IT/ITES industries, Sushant is currently associated with eClerx Services Ltd. He ventured into the field of literature approximately five years ago as a blogger and storyteller and officially launched his career as an author in January 2024.

His literary work and professional achievements have been widely recognized with numerous prestigious awards, including:

- 'Asia's Most Promising Professional Skills Trainer and Inspiring Writer Award' by Asia Awards powered by World Research Congress (WRC)
- Conferred with the 'Bharat Vibhushan Puraskar 2024' for his book, honored as the 'Best Self-

Help Book of the Year for Students and Young Professionals.'

- Awarded with Rabindranath Tagore Literature Award by DRDC
- Indo-British Literary Award from The Authors of India (T.A.O.I)
- Recognized as the 'Most Inspiring Author, Professional Skills Trainer, and Motivational Speaker' at the 'India Icon Awards 2024' (India Business Awards).
- Featured as one of the 'Top 5 Writers of 2024' by Mid-Day.

Sushant is also a dedicated educator, serving as a visiting faculty member and corporate mentor for MBA students. He brings a unique blend of theoretical expertise and practical insights to both his writing and teaching.

You can reach out to him at- sushant_krajput@yahoo.co.uk

Website - **www.sushantrajput.co.in**